ESTALILLA KABAROAN ESKRIMA

ESTALILLA KABAROAN ESKRIMA

OVERVIEW OF THE 3-PART SYSTEM

RAMIRO U. ESTALILLA JR.

www.TambuliMedia.com
Spring House, PA USA

DISCLAIMER

The author and publisher of this book DISCLAIM ANY RESPONSIBILITY over any injury as a result of the techniques taught in this book. Readers are advised to consult a physician about their physical condition before undergoing any strenuous training or dangerous physical activity. This is a martial arts book and details dangerous techniques that can cause serious physical injury and even death. Practice and training require a fit and healthy student and a qualified instructor.

ISBN-10: 1-943155-27-5
ISBN-13: 978-1-943155-27-9

Edited by Ronald Reekers
Copy Editor: Jody Amato
Photo Editor: Tyler R. Rea
Interior and Cover Design by Summer Bonne

DEDICATION

This work is sincerely dedicated to all my past, current, and future students in loving memory of my parents, Ramiro A. Estalilla Sr. and Aurelia U. Estalilla, who taught the skills of their martial arts heritage for noble purposes, good motives, and peaceful intentions.

—Ramiro A. Estalilla, Sr.

Ramiro A. Estalilla, Sr.

Four Generations: Ramiro Estalilla, Ramiro Jr., Prince and Jace Estalilla

TESTIMONIALS

"Grand Master Estalilla is a true master. He embodies all of the qualities that I aspire to as a martial artist and as a person. Apo is the most generous and knowledgeable teacher I have ever trained with. His skill in Escrima is truly amazing, and the love he has for all his students has created a true Kabaroan."

—**Robert Allen White, Associate Grandmaster Kabaroan**

"Nothing compares to time with Apo. He calls himself the youngest Grandmaster, since he has no teeth. To know him and train with him, you can't help but love him. Shihan Evans, thanks for bringing us together nearly twenty-five years ago."

—**Edward Bansuelo, Associate Grandmaster Kabaroan**

"I truly love this man. There are martial artists, and then there are men like Apo. He sets the standard we should all try to meet."

—**Wade Williams, Associate Grandmaster Kabaroan**

"To me, Grandmaster Estalilla Jr. is a teacher's teacher. His art of Kabaroan is very systematic, direct, and to the point. It has the ability to be added to any martial arts you already know or can stand on its own. I am forever grateful for the knowledge he has passed down to myself and shared with my students."

—**Gerald Beardsley, Associate Grandmaster Kabaroan**

"If you have spent any time training under Apo Ramiro, one of the first things you learn is how humble and soft-spoken he is. The lessons he imparts to students, both novice and advanced, not only deal with Kabaroan, the martial arts, but also with life and Christianity: being a good person and giving praise to both God and Jesus."

—**Anthony Manansala, Associate Grandmaster Kabaroan**

"Learning Kabaroan has been a blessing for me. Grandmaster Estalilla has taught me something greater than physical skill. He and the other instructors under him have helped change my life through their influences of showing good character. They helped pull me from the gang life I once lived in and helped me return to God and family. I will always be in debt to Apo. Thank you and God bless."

—**Edward Almaguer, Associate Grandmaster Kabaroan**

"Grand Master Estalilla has been both a mentor to me in the Filipino martial arts and a father figure. I love that he is a minister of the Gospel of Jesus Christ. I have been a youth pastor in the past, so we also have this as a common bond. In Shorin-Ryu Karate, an Okinawan martial art that I have studied for more than forty-two years, there is a title, which translated means "a model for others." If such a title exists in the Filipino martial arts, then I can think of no one who exemplifies this better than Grand Master Ramiro U. Estalilla Jr. He is truly my model for what a martial arts teacher and grand master should be."

—**Tim Evans, Associate Grandmaster Kabaroan**

"I have had the privilege of working with quite a few masters and grand masters of their particular arts, and I can say without a doubt that Apo Estalilla is one of the most open, giving, and caring instructors I have ever worked with. His influence on my life has been great and his teachings have helped me both as a person and as a martial artist. He has so much to give each and every time I get the honor of working with him and I am so thankful for the depth of knowledge and application his art has provided me and mine. I am blessed to be able to call him my instructor, teacher, mentor, and friend."

—**Dennis Forleo, Shepherd-Warrior Martial Arts, Billings, Montana**

"Grandmaster Ramiro has been a great influence on my son and me. He gave us daily guidance in improving ourselves, being humble, and enlarging our circle of friends."

—**Jaime Vicitacion, Associate Grandmaster Kabaroan**

ACKNOWLEDGMENTS

Beyond my ability to express in words, I wish to acknowledge my great debt of gratitude to several persons. Without them this book, which began as notes for a handbook or manual almost fifty years ago, would not have been completed.

For their constructive criticism, valuable suggestions, moral and technical support, patience and tolerance, various skills and assistance, guidance, and inspiration:

To my wife, Flordeliza, my son, Prince, my daughters, Alpha and Brenda.

To all my students—past, current, and future.

To all my teachers, peers, associates, and fellow martial artists.

Estalilla Family Portrait

TABLE OF CONTENTS

PUBLISHER'S FOREWORD

For nearly 25 years I have been a student of Grandmaster Ramiro Estalilla, whom we student lovingly refer to Apo. He is a kind and loving man with a huge heart, and I am proud to represent him and his art in my own small way. I initially reached out to Apo in 1993, just before the publication of my first book on eskrima, titled *Filipino Martial Arts: Cabales Serrada Escrima*. I was working on my next book and had also begun a newsletter, titled *Tambuli* (which 20 years later I revived in name and spirit as the name of my publishing company). I had seen an article in *Black Belt* magazine about Apo and his Kabaroan style which intrigued me, and I wanted to know more. So I got his number through a mutual friend and called him. After this call, we became friends. And soon thereafter, I flew out to Fresno, CA to meet him and become his student.

What I find intriguing about Kabaroan Eskrima is how unique it is among Filipino martial arts. There are hundreds of different FMA styles, but most share a common use of stick and swords of between 24-inches and 32-inches. Kabaroan makes use of much

Ramiro Estalilla and Mark Wiley Ca. 1994

longer and heavier sticks; poles really. And these poles are representations of staff, spear and shield. These are weapons of traditional cultures used throughout the Philippines, not of the modern-era stick and knife and bolo methods. The weapons are held at different lengths, one used to propel the other in various directions, another used as a shield, another method to extend its length during projection. It is a unique FMA to watch and practice.

Moreover, the Estalilla Kabaroan method approaches the sinawali training from a different perspective. It utilized methods of "merging" the weapons over "meeting" them in force. Additionally, the breakdown of the art into techniques of Sensilla, Bambolia and Compuesta with methods known as Tiradin and Todasan, also make this FMA unique.

We owe a debt of gratitude for men like GM Ramiro Estalilla, who is also a fencer and a minister and who has never bragged of defeating foes or surviving death matches. With his humility, and generous nature, comes the guardian of an older and mostly unseen Filipino martial art: Kabaroan. I think it was in 1997 that Apo and I began working together on this book, while I was martial arts editor at Tuttle Publishing. He kept saying, "This is my life's work, it must be complete." And so, 20 years later he has indeed produced a book worthy of a lifetime of thought and effort.

It is with honor that I am able to publish this authoritative overview of the art of Kabaroan Eskrima, by my dear friend, mentor and teacher, Ramiro U. Estalilla, Jr. We are both indebted to Associate Grand Master Ron Reekers, for pulling it all together for publication and to Guro Dan Inosanto for providing a Foreword.

Dr. Mark Wiley
Publisher, Tambuli Media
President, Integrated Eskrima International
Vice-President, Arnis Pederaasyong Internasyonal (iArnis)
Senior Advisor, Mataw Guro Association
Associate Grand Master, Estalilla Kabaroan Eskrima

FOREWORD

BY GRANDMASTER DAN INOSANTO

It is an honor to write this foreword for my teacher and friend, Grandmaster Ramiro Estalilla Jr.'s new book, *Kabaroan Eskrima*.

I have had the privilege of being Grand Master Estalilla's student for more than twenty years.

I first met Grand Master Estalilla at the Fountain Valley School of Ronald Reekers. I was impressed not only by his skill and knowledge in Estalilla Eskrima, but also impressed by the man. It is rare you find a man, martial artist, and expert in his field who is so genuinely humble, kind, and giving.

Grand Master Estalilla is man of great faith, a minister whose love and dedication to his Christian principles is never lost as he teaches and trains his students not only techniques, but culture and history.

Captions: Guro Danny Inosanto and Grand Master Ramiro Estalilla Jr., circa 1995 – 2015
Photos provided and copyright of The Inosanto Academy

Training with Grand Master Estalilla has made his students more proficient martial artists, and if they follow his example of humility, love, and kindness, it has helped make them better human beings.

I highly recommend this book, *Estalilla Kabaroan*, to all students in the Filipino martial arts. This book will be great addition to your training and understanding of Estalilla Kabaroan.

**Associate Grand Master
Dan Inosanto**
Founder and Head Instructor,
The Inosanto Academy of Martial Arts
Marina del Rey, California

INTRODUCTION

The Philippines is an archipelagic nation made up of 7,107 islands that span 1,840 kilometers north to south. With a land area of 300,780 square kilometers, the Philippines is considered a medium-sized nation, about the size of its first colonizer, Spain, and a little larger than the British Isles. The three main island groups are Luzon (Northern), Visayas (Central), and Mindanao (Southern). There are 100 identified tribal dialects and languages.

The Ilocano-speaking tribe is one of the ten largest. Ilocanos live in Northern and Central Luzon and in many parts of Mindanao and Palawan. The great number of tribes naturally accounts for the numerous styles or systems of fighting arts with hand weapons.

The purpose of this volume is to introduce the Luzonian and Ilocano system, including those similarly practiced by some in the Visayas and by those who speak Maguindanao and Visayans in Southern Philippines who carried on or practiced Lapulapu's system.

The popularity of Kali, Eskrima, and Arnis in the world of martial arts has led many earnest fans and practitioners to think that Kabaroan is one style or system offered by Filipinos. Because of that, many persons have used the term "Kabaroan" as though it were a style or system of Eskrima. Kali, too, has been treated by some well-meaning exponents to be different from Eskrima and Arnis.

However, I look at them all as one and the same art, with varying emphases and differing techniques. Therefore, I use them synonymously and interchangeably. Some terms are older than others, and some have other methods or ways of executions, but they all fall under the general category of armasan (weaponry, or defenses with weapons), otherwise called "armas de mano" (weapons of the hand). Naturally, in this category, Kabaroan is a system and a style of martial art. It is unique, however: Kabaroan is both the title of the artist (practitioner) as well as the name of the art. In other words, I can correctly say that I am a Kabaroan, and I practice (the art of) Kabaroan.

The scope of this volume is limited to the first two parts, or subsystems, of Kabaroan: Sencilla and Bambolia, although reference is made to the third part, Compuesta, in the definitions and outlines of Kabaroan.

This work will focus on matters that are not found or fully treated in existing books and videos on Eskrima. A brief history, philosophy, principles, and definitions will be given, but stances, postures, exercises without weapons, and detailed types of weapons will be omitted since they abound in other Eskrima books and martial arts publications. This book will, therefore, complement or supplement prevailing works on the art.

The presentation here is designed to be systematic for quick, simple, and easy reference on Kabaroan. All materials are original, as they were taught to me from the time I started learning at age eleven, during the outbreak of World War II. Those times were unlike the previous years of my childhood (ages six to ten) when, out of childhood amazement and curiosity, I used to watch my father teach estoque. The war years were times of trouble that demanded a serious study of armas de mano for family and neighborhood protection and preservation against enemies from many sides.

I started writing down notes on Eskrima at age sixteen, just after the war, when I was a high school freshman in Cotabato, Mindanao, and began to study Kabaroan from my uncle (my mother's first cousin), Bernardo U. Banay in Pagadian, Zamboanga. Uncle Bandong was my father's top student of Kabaroan way back in Luzon before 1936. The final phase of this writing took place in California after fifty years in the firing line of studying, practicing, teaching, and refining the art, and compiling, writing, and rewriting this body of knowledge.

This work is divided into four sections. Section I, the first three chapters, deal with historical and cultural matters and principles. Section II, chapters four to nine, discuss the basics: terms, strikes, defenses, disarms, counters, exercises, and forms with dances. Section III, chapters ten and eleven, include biographical information and notes. Section IV contains appendices that provide supplementary materials for students and teachers alike.

Many of the terms used are in English, Ilocano, Spanish, Tagalog, and Visayan. Where possible, they are translated or transliterated into English or given equivalent meanings. Some terms are coined words, others are contracted, and still others are acronyms. A complete glossary of terms used in Kabaroan is given in the appendix.

The phrase "For every technique there is a counter-technique" is almost absolutely true in Kabaroan. The options for and against a weapon technique are so many and seem to be inexhaustible. One must learn and understand the principle underlying a technique.

Examples are given and the rest can be discovered or invented by the learner. Allowance is given for the joy of discovery and invention.

Whether or not Kabaroan is a style or system of Eskrima does not really matter. And no claim is made that Kabaroan is better than others. I just believe that Kabaroan holds some aces, which are offered to those willing and able to learn something new, and which are probably different from but compatible with almost every fighting art and system of discipline.

SECTION I

Overview of Kabaoran

CHAPTER 1

Introduction to Kabaroan

Kabaroan is the Filipino martial art and system of fencing and self-defense. Specifically, it is the traditional way of fighting with hand weapons or hand-arms (armas de mano), such as bolos, swords called kampilans (cutlasses), spears, iron-wood sticks, and fire-hardened staves, as opposed to fighting with handguns or firearms (armas de fuego), such as pistols, rifles, and revolvers.

I have taught and practiced Kabaroan publicly and privately as a martial art course for physical fitness and self-defense. The training course demonstrates the art hidden and preserved in folk dances, its basic principles, history and philosophy, and its exercises and disciplines for fitness, health, and fun.

Historical and Cultural Background

From a cultural approach, I would like to share and pass on the fighting arts practiced by Filipinos long before Rajah Lalulapu defeated Ferdinand Magellan in the Battle of Mactan in 1521, and long before Marco Polo visited the Philippines around ad 1300.

The Filipinos, like other people and nations, are a freedom-loving people. Their history and struggle for liberty is full of battles—both internally among themselves and externally against foreign invaders. Their love for freedom is evidenced by their highly systematized fighting arts and by the hundreds of fighting weapons with which they have defended themselves.

What is known today as Kali, Eskrima, or Arnis is the popular segment and integral part of the Filipinos' fighting arts. Before the Philippines was discovered by Europeans, or rediscovered by the Western World, the Filipinos had been practicing their martial arts and self-defense systems—from Lapulapu to the revolt against Spain (1521 to 1896); from Mactan to Bataan, down to the liberation and independence of 1946.

During the World War II staged and fought in Asia, the famous "Bolo Battalions," which consisted of well-trained Filipino fighters equipped primarily with bladed weapons, swooped into enemy camps and raided their garrisons in the still of the nights. The raids were romantically referred to as serenades with blades, rifles and grenades.

The martial arts (plural due to various styles) were practiced by leaders of the Philippine Revolution against Spain, viz: Dr. Jose P. Rizal, the national hero; by Andres Bonifacio, the leader of the Katipunan society; by General Emilio Aguinaldo, who became the President of the First Philippine Republic; by Bishop Gregorio Aglipay, the revolutionary priest; by General Antonio Luna with his sparring partner in fencing, Major Eusebio Estalilla, just to name a few.

The fighting arts were employed by myriads of valiant heroes, veterans, and defenders of many wars against foreign invaders and domestic marauders.

The word "Eskrima" comes from Spanish "esgrima", which means swordsmanship. This term evolved from a Latin/German word translated "skirmish". Derived from it are the words scrimmage and scrummage.

The art of Kali, Eskrima, or Arnis is known by other names among Filipinos. The Tagalogs call it Pananandata, and Arnis. The Visayans call it Kaliradman, Pang-olisi, Botho-an, and Escrima. The Pampanguenos call it Sinawali; the Pangasinans call it Kalirongan. The Ilocanos have several names for it: Kabaroan, Panagigam, Armasan, Estoque, Estocada, Garrote-an, Eskrima, Armas de Mano, Dalan ti Armas, Pinnang-oran, Tinnagbatan, Minnalloan, etc.

Outlawed but Preserved

In 1764, the practice of Eskrima began to decline. It was outlawed and forbidden by authorities during the Spanish regime. Filipinos who practiced Kali were branded as bandits and outlaws. It was claimed that the arts were too brutal. They led to death of practitioners who had gone out of control. It was also said that Filipinos were so engrossed with their practice that they neglected to work on their farms. The apparent reason behind the prohibition, however, was the fear by the authorities that the Filipinos were preparing to revolt against the government.

The outlawing and prohibition of the martial art constrained and compelled the Filipinos to practice Kali, Arnis, or Eskrima in secrecy. The brave ones were forced to practice in hiding, and when the "guardia civil" (civil guards) made their rounds to catch violators, the practitioners had already resorted to folk dances. As soon as the roving policemen left, having seen that the Filipinos were simply doing traditional folk dances, the dancing martial artists immediately resumed to practice the forbidden art.

Some Filipinos practiced the arts under the canopy of darkness, and others under the moonlight or starry nights. The forms and movements of Filipino folk dances, such us the Carinosa, Sakuting, Tinikling, and other dances as we know them today, showed distinct marks and influence of the fighting arts of Kabaroan.

Goals and Objectives

Kabaroan is a martial art and brutal as a fighting system; therefore our cultural objective is to humanize the art, to civilize the artist, and to refine the system.

I hope that all practitioners, both students and teachers, will learn from the start to practice the art with maximum safety; that despite whatever motivated them to study Kabaroan (and other martial arts for that matter), they would align themselves with those who have committed to study, practice, and teach it for peaceful intentions and for the good of humanity, so that our world might become a better and safer place in which to live.

Kabaroan is Dynamic

The art of Eskrima deals with human energy and force in motion, and it is vigorous and productive. More than that, it is geared toward a cultural approach.

Kali, the older name for Kabaroan, Eskrima, or Arnis, was the popular sport and martial art before Ferdinand Magellan (Fernando Magallanes) discovered the Philippines on April 7, 1521. The Portuguese explorer, who worked for King Phillip (Felipe) of Spain, was the commander of the expedition, and later named the islands after Phillip. It is also reasonable to believe that Kali must have been the art and sport before Marco Polo visited the islands.

Historically, the martial art is linked with many bloody battles fought by Filipinos. Among them is the battle on April 27, 1521, on the shores of Mactan Island, off the coast of Cebu, central Philippines. The defending warriors (Gubators) used bolos, kampilans, sun-dried and fire-tempered wooden lances, staffs and spears. Rajah (prince or chief) Lapulapu and his native defenders fought the invaders with armas de mano in hand-to-hand mortal combats. Magellan and many of his Spanish soldiers were slain.

What Kabaroan Offers

Kabaroan has unique self-defense features. Primarily, it is practiced and promoted today because of its cultural and sports values, with its calisthenic and exercise values for physical fitness, and secondarily, for its self-defense merits. In a cultural approach to martial arts, the aim in Kabaroan is to humanize, not animalize, the art; to civilize, not barbarize, the artist; and to refine, not coarsen, the system.

Eskrima offers physical, mental and inner discipline benefits. For the youth, it offers very rewarding exercises that help develop mental alertness and physical agility. It offers a wholesome sports competition and is a very safe combative art. For women, children, and senior citizens, Arnis offers nonstrenuous, nonrigorous, and moderate exercises for physical fitness, muscle toning, self-discipline, self-confidence, and figure control. Kali also offers basic, easy, practical, and effective defense techniques for self, family, and neighborhood.

Kabaroan is Safe

Today, under controlled practices, Kabaroan is very safe sport. It is safer than fencing with foil, epee, or saber—even without protective covers for the head, body, hands, and feet. But for maximum safety and to prevent accidents, extreme precaution must be undertaken. Under guided instructions and controlled practice situations, the art uses not only light rattans and wooden swords, but also foam-padded plastic or wooden sticks in lieu of bladed weapons, bolos, or swords. Sometimes, real blades are used by teachers, experts, or advance students in rare but pure exhibition of the art.

Big Stick Rules of Safety

In Kabaroan, control is the basic rule of safety in all methods of practice. It must prevail in calisthenic, sportive, and combative Eskrima. Control must govern and dominate the attitude and action of Arnis players or Eskrimadors. The practitioner must, first of all, discipline himself to subjugate his own spirit, mind, and body. Self-control and self-discipline are indispensable in Kabaroan sportsmanship.

There are three big words beginning with "s" to remember in safely practicing "big stick Eskrima", namely: **S**elf-control, **S**imulation and **S**low motion. After some time of practice, beginners develop accuracy and better striking techniques, and gradually increase speed. "Control" is the keyword. Even when simulating a strong strike, players should continue to exercise control. Every practitioner, whether beginner, intermediate, or advanced, should begin slowly in learning new techniques, gradually developing speed with accuracy. Every situation must be under control, and the Eskrimador must always be in control.

Prevent and avoid accidents. Follow the rules of safety and you can't go wrong; neglect them and you can't go right.

Code of Honor and Rules of Conduct

To ensure maximum safety in the practice of Filipino martial arts, the following Code of Honor and Rules of Conduct have been adopted:

* I will conduct myself with the utmost care and highest respect.
* I will control and guard my speech, temper, and spirit, as well as my strikes and defenses.
* I will not provoke others, and I will not be easily provoked to anger.
* I will be honest, fair, and constructive in my opinions, appreciation, or criticism of the abilities of my fellow students, members, or teachers.
* I will respect and protect the honor and dignity of others, as I would like them to respect and protect mine.
* I will follow the Golden Rule.
* If I violate this Code of Honor and Rules of Conduct, full responsibility will be mine.
* On my word of honor, so help me, God.

CHAPTER 2

Kabaroan Origins

"No matter how deadly your art and style may be, you must control your strikes within the sphere of good motives against a background of peaceful intentions."
—Ramiro Abellera Estalilla Sr.

Kabaroan is a composite style or system of the Filipino martial art that utilizes bigger, longer, and heavier weapons without excluding smaller, shorter, and lighter ones. Hence, the phrase "big stick Eskrima" usually refers to Kabaroan.

The word "Kabaroan" has several meanings:

* As the superlative degree of the adjective "baro" (new), it means the newest, latest, modern;

* As living, existing, or coming into being during the same period of time; belonging to the same age group, society, coequal;

* As a coined or compound word from "Ka" and "Baroang." it means "Sir" or "Lord Baron". As a system of fighting art named after the barons and better known as Eskrima, Kali, or Arnis, it is the system popular among the Ilocanos.

It is also described as Armasan, Panagigam, and Dalan ti Armas, among other terms. The long style was popular among some Visayans, who perpetuated and carried on Lapulapu's system instead of Rajah Humabon's. (King Humabon of Cebu was the chieftain who befriended the foreign invaders. Lapulapu withstood and fought them.)

When Kabaroan resurfaced or was reintroduced before the 1900s, it was meant to reinforce, improve, and refine the prevailing styles. However, when it was taught, students and teachers alike received it as a new system. One may ask, "How do we account for the similarity between Kabaroan as practiced by the Ilocos regions of Luzon and those who carried on Lapulapu's system of utilizing bigger, longer, and heavier weapons?"

The first theory is that they have a common source. There were others who sailed from the Indonesian Peninsula or from Borneo but were probably driven by the winds, and so they landed in the Visayan Islands and others landed in Luzon. The other theory is that the Ilocos regions were influenced by Chinese traders in the Northern Philippines. The Luzonians had good trade relations with the merchants on junks (boats). Encounters resulting from misunderstandings cannot be ruled out to have had affected Filipino martial arts practices and systems.

Kabaroan Practice Methods

Eskrima has few types of practice methods, namely:

Follow the Leader — This is the demonstration of forms, strikes, and defenses, movements of head and body, hands and feet, parrying and evasions, steps and positions, individually or collectively. In action, the teacher leads and the student follow.

Prearranged Drill — This involves planned and controlled strikes and defenses that are made in repetitive drills. Two protagonists, as partners, go through a pattern of offense and defense techniques, demonstrating and executing forms and skills. Controlled contacts by partners are made more often than not.

Freestyle Solo — In this method, the individual player demonstrates forms, styles, striking and defending techniques against an *imaginary* opponent. Emphasis is on artistic forms and refinement of execution in the performance of Arnistic dance.

Freestyle Bout — In this method, protagonists display highly controlled strikes and defenses, but draw from their individual resources, from their wealth of knowledge and skills, training and experience, with or without armor.

Points in bout competition are scored when a hit (touch—actual or virtual) is made to any part of the body, head, hands, feet, or when one is disarmed. Disarming without hurting an opponent is the most ideal objective and highly commendable, receiving double points. A disarmed person is like an unarmed opponent. Striking a disarmed opponent is like striking a helpless person and is to be discouraged and avoided, unless expressly and explicitly agreed upon by the combatants to continue the competition unarmed.

Kabaroan's Basic Goals

The basic and primary goals of Arnis or Eskrima are:

Calisthenic — Eskrima is primarily intended for physical fitness. It aims to develop rhythm, coordination, alertness, dexterity, speed, and strength, and beauty of figure, with the ultimate goal being a healthy body, mind, and spirit.

Sportive — Eskrima includes calisthenic objectives and is geared toward safe, honorable, intramural competition within respective ranks, styles, and schools. Promotions and rankings are in order as a result of just and fair testings and/or competitions.

Combative — Eskrima projects beyond these and encompasses the goals of calisthenic and sportive Eskrimas. It anticipates a defense for the honor and safety of the country, family, another person, or oneself. Dignity is at stake, and a life is in jeopardy. It calls for self-defense.

Kabaroan Blends With Other Arts

Eskrima lends itself so easily to other forms of martial arts. Akin to many, if not all of them, it adapts to and integrates with them. It uses the same principles and techniques of martial arts such as aikido, boxing, combato, capoeira, gungfu, judo, jujitsu, karate, kendo, kempo, kenpo, kungfu, penjak silat, taichi, taekwondo, Thai boxing, wing chun, savate, and others. Eskrima extends to, and is the extension of, other martial arts. It can be an art within an art; it is very compatible with them.

Present-day Kabaroan has been systematized, safety-geared, modernized, and synthesized from related martial arts. It has inherited, retained, and offers to pass on the essentials (techniques, philosophies, styles, and forms) of the ancient Filipino sports and martial arts.

Subsystems of Kabaroan

Learning the Filipino terms is optional, but it is important to know some basic English terms, which are contractions, abbreviations, or acronyms. Filipino and Spanish terms are given English meanings, equivalents, or translations where possible. Some native words have been anglicized or transliterated to preserve the root where their meanings or translations are neither possible nor apparent.

On the method of handling or gripping weapons, Kabaroan may be divided into three categories or subsystems: Sencilla, Bambolia, and Compuesta.

SENCILLA (ONE-HANDED SINGLE WEAPON SYSTEM)

* Short Stick or Knife (26" or less)

* Walking Cane (36" more or less)

* Walking Staff (50" more or less)

* Long Staff (60" more or less)

BAMBOLIA (TWO-HANDED SINGLE WEAPON SYSTEM)

* Short Stick (26" or more)

* Medium Length Baton (36" to 39")

* Walking Staff (50" more or less)

* Long Staff (Spear Length, 60" more or less)

COMPUESTA (TWO-HANDED DOUBLE WEAPON SYSTEM)

* Double Dagger or Short Sticks (9" to 18")

* Double Baton or Sword (26" to 36")

* Long and Short Sticks (Sword and Dagger)

* Shield Staff (Bangkao) and Baton or Spear (40" more or less)

Parts of the Stick and How to Hold It

The following is for standard riot-control (truncheon) stick and walking staff. Proportionate adjustment should be made for shorter sticks.

* Grip section—the first quarter of either end of baton.

* Butt section—the first eight of either end of baton.

* Gore/Thrust section—the tip or point of either end of baton.

* Graze/Score section—the edge of either end of baton.

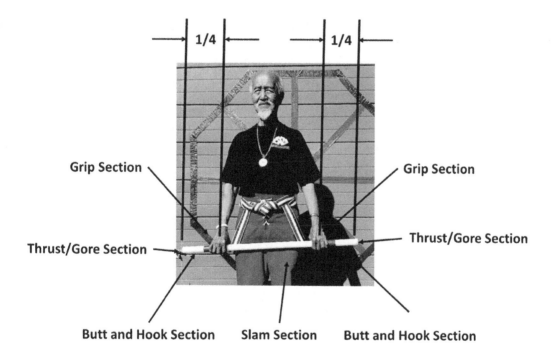

* Slam/Push/Ram section—the middle portion (shaft) of baton.

* Hook/Disarm section—the butt and grip quarters of baton.

* Defense section—the second, third, and fourth quarters of baton.

Target Areas for the Stick

From the viewpoint of law enforcement, impact weapons such as the baton stick and the truncheon come under California Penal Code Section 12020. Impact weapons may bring civil and criminal liability. Therefore, the target areas of impact weapons are of vital importance and concern to law enforcement officers, who carry nightsticks, batons, and the truncheon.

Strikes should be controlled to show care and prudence. Uncontrolled strikes with any police baton, whether lightweight or heavyweight, are painful, dangerous, and deadly. Whether we have the law on our side, or we are on the side of the law, consider the target areas and consequences of our strikes with impact weapons. Should the target of your strike be tragic?

Lethal areas are the least targeted: head, temple, face, neck, chest, torso, ribs, and groin. Blows to these areas may cause death or severe permanent injury. Caution areas are secondary targets only in grave assaults: hands, elbows, knees, feet, shoulder blades, and all joints. Blows may cause immobilization or disruption of motor functions. Painful areas are primary targets: any mass tissue such as the forearms, biceps, buttocks, calves, thighs, legs, and stomach. These blows will cause temporary pain.

Methods of Weapon Grip

Sencilla (Simple, Single)—
One-Handed Grip

Bambolia (Super Strike)—Two-Handed Grip

Compuesta (Composite, Compound)—Double Weapon Grip

Tiradin and Todasan: Two Sides of One Coin

Kabaroan falls under the category of armas de mano. Each of the three divisions or methods of handling weapons—Sencilla, Bambolia, and Compuesta—employs Tiradin and Todasan as two defensive patterns or systems of parrying or deflection. In turn, deflection, which is closely executed with evasion, operates either by meeting or blocking (called pasabat) or by merging and blending (called paayon).

In defense training, Tiradin and Todasan are referred to as two systems or schools of thought. As a native Filipino term, "Tiradin" simply means "hit back, strike too." "Todasan", on the other hand, implies a total or complete action to the finish, to the end, until all and everything is over. It means to finish off, exterminate, eliminate, and fully destroy.

Tiradin and Todasan, however, are used here as acronyms (while retaining their original and basic meanings) for some ideas and practices in Filipino martial arts and some sports. Both terms, therefore, are given and have acquired deeper, broader, and technical meanings.

TIRADIN is an acronym that stands for "Training In Regular Armed Defenses, Instructions, and Novelties." It is the popular system and common practice of defense by meeting and blocking every strike. It is a force against force (pasabat). All defensive strikes come from the opposite side or direction. TIRADIN is the system of strikes and defenses commonly and generally associated with blocking and meeting force against force, as opposed to TODASAN.

TODASAN is an acronym that stands for "Tactical Offensive Defenses Against Systematic Assaults and Nuisances." It is the unpopular, unique system and uncommon practice of defense by merging and blending with every strike. It is a going with the force (paayon). All defensive strikes come from the same side or direction. TODASAN is the system of strikes and defenses especially or specifically identified and associated with blending, merging, and going with the force, as opposed to TIRADIN.

Both TIRADIN and TODASAN are needful and useful. They are like the two hands of a person; the oars on each side of a canoe, kayak, or boat; or like the two parts of the Bible, the Old and New Testaments. As a system, TIRADIN represents the old, and TODASAN represents the new. The old is revealed and current in the new; the new was concealed and latent in the old. In like manner, TODASAN was hidden and covered in TIRADIN, but TIRADIN is shown and uncovered in TODASAN. (Some readers of the scriptures understand this relationship between the two covenants.)

As an offensive technique, TIRADIN is primarily a force against force, while TODASAN is generally a going with a force. As a defensive technique, TIRADIN is basically blocking and meeting a force, whereas TODASAN is generally a blending and merging with a force. Like music, TIRADIN is lively, flashy and rhythmic, while TODASAN is deadly, terrible, and offbeat. The one is (or can be) theatrical and stage oriented; the other is non-flashy and off-stage oriented. The former can be playfully comical or amusing, whereas the latter is dreadfully brutal or frightening.

A Balanced System

Defense-wise, TIRADIN and TODASAN constitute the whole Kabaroan system. One is not exclusive of the other. Rather, they complement and supplement each other, and form a balanced system. To learn, practice, and teach Kabaroan is to maintain both TIRADIN and TODASAN. Nevertheless, whatever one's background, experience, system, or style, welcome to the study of the Filipino martial arts. A new art would do a person well—in body, heart, and soul.

CHAPTER 3

Fundamental Principles

It is only natural that my Biblical education, religious training, and spiritual experience have influenced my philosophy and practice of martial arts in general and the Filipino Dalan ti Armas (way of hand weapons) in particular. As a Christian minister and Bible teacher without being preachy, and Eskrima practitioner, I believe and advocate in being "at peace with" and in "doing good to" all persons. Naturally, as martial artist and eskrimador, my life, teachings, and practices reflect and are governed by the two great moral principles, to wit:

The Principle of Life

Life is sacred. This is a basic, underlying, and a priori principle. No person has the right to take another person's life. That prerogative belongs only to the creator and giver of life—Jehovah Ehohim or Yahweh Elohim. We address Him reverently as Lord God.

The right to live must be respected. Disrespect for life is a disregard for God who commanded, "Thou shall not kill." Because life is sacred, the law is moral and eternal. No person should take the law into their own hands. Great care and prudence, therefore, must be taken and exercised by the eskrimador, kalidor, arnisador, gubator (warrior) or any martial artist in practice, sports, and combat. The life of the opponent must be safeguarded and protected, as well as yours.

The Principle of Love

Love you neighbor as yourself. This is corollary to the Principle of Life, and expresses itself in two ways: the positive Golden Rule, "Do unto others as you would have that others do unto you." and the negative Golden Rule, "Do not unto others what you would not that others do unto you."

The Golden Rule (The Moral Principle)

When this principle is corrupted or violated, we harm others and ourselves too. If we bring any sorrow, grief, or pain upon others, we also bring ill will, hatred, or unhappiness upon ourselves. When any of these happen, we violate the Principle of Love.

Jesus Christ, the greatest teacher of all time that the world has ever known, taught his disciples and students, "Love your enemies." He also commanded them to love one another as He loves them. It is the highest degree of love that He speaks of when He said:

"Greater love hath no man than this; that a man lay down his life for his friends."
—New Testament (John 15:12, 13)

It is no wonder that love and life prevail as great dominant themes in such passage as:

"God loved the world so much that he gave his only-begotten Son, Jesus Christ, in order that anyone who will believe in Him should not perish but have life forever."
—New Testament (John 3:16, 36)

Great Ideals Derived From Principles

Respect and Honor. Treat your opponent as your equal in ability, even if the person is your enemy. Respect and honor is the least that you can give, even if you defeat and not bury him.

Honesty and Sincerity. Honesty is the best policy. Sincerity without flattery in appreciation is like white snow on a mountaintop.

Control and Discipline.	No matter how deadly your art and style may be, you must control your strikes within the sphere of good motives against a background of peaceful intentions.
Faith and Confidence.	Faith and confidence in others, as in ourselves, simply reflect and speak of inner experiences with someone higher than ourselves.
Character and Conduct.	Our character is what we really are and will show itself in our conduct toward or dealing with others.
Loyalty and Integrity.	Be loyal to your friends and country, but before enemies, keep your integrity.
Humility and Pride.	Maintain a balance between your pride and humility; have pride but don't be haughty, and be humble when you are naughty.
Mercy and Courage.	With all our ability and courage, let us not fail to have mercy, for someday we may beg for one.
Gentleness and Appreciation.	Gentleness is the mark of a gentleman, and appreciation from him is like a trophy.
Friendship.	Use your art to enlarge your circle of friends and not to create a band of enemies. Remember, your worst enemy could be your best friend, who would betray and turn against you, and become another Judas Iscariot.
Sportsmanship.	In this life, sometimes you win, sometimes you lose. Life is a give and take, for no man is an island.
Fairness and Justice.	Every person who feels discriminated against and unjustly treated longs for the scale of justice and fair treatment, and somehow expresses the substance of the Golden Rule.

Levels of Forces and Types of Weapons

Modern practitioners, authorities, and writers seem to agree and have identified four degrees or levels of forces. The type of weapons or arms to employ must achieve the level or degree of force desired. In the previous decades or centuries, there were just two types or kinds of weapons or arms: weapons of the hand (armas de mano), and firearms (armas de fuego).

In current times, however, world citizens recognize, emphasize, and demand respect for human rights. We are also compelled, by force of necessity and moral responsibility, to acknowledge and include the power of reason or words (armas de palabra; power of negotiation and persuasion), and empty hand or weaponless techniques (armas de nada) as additional tools.

FORCE OF WORDS (POWER OF PERSUASION)

These four types of weapons or arms match and correspond perfectly with four identified levels of forces. The force of words comes under the power of reason in the attempts to use persuasion and negotiation first of all, before any other force is employed.

MINIMUM FORCE (EMPTY HAND; WEAPONLESS)

Where the first fails, minimum force is contemplated with empty-hand or weaponless techniques. Warning: even a minimum force and weaponless, empty-hand technique can be lethal.

MEDIUM FORCE (HAND WEAPONS)

If the first two levels of forces and types of arms or weapons are deemed risky or unsuitable for the situation under consideration, then the medium force with hand arms or weapons would probably be employed.

MAXIMUM FORCE (FIREARMS)

Then, as a last recourse, where justified and deemed necessary, the maximum force of firearms, along and combined with or apart from the other types of weapons and levels of forces, may be used.

Eskrima as a Weapon-based System

The reasoning behind the weapon-based concept is that weapons are simply the extension of the hands. In times of war, nobody goes to battle empty-handed or without weapons. Whether fights are over trivial matters, tribal squabbles, or against foreign invaders, nobody goes to war with empty hands.

It is probably a wishful thinking and modern-day belief system, or maybe a theory of battle strategy by a number of martial artists who teach and insist on an idealistic concept, that people went to fight in battles all empty-handed—totally weaponless (awanigam).

To Kabaroan, the above theory is simply too basic to be accepted or believed. There are a lot of carabaos, or water buffalos, but not many cows and bulls, in many countries where martial arts are taught with those systems, strategies, and sciences as bedtime or bonfire stories.

According to Biblical history, as Goliath mocked David, who went to fight the ten-foot giant Gath of the Philistine army with a stone and a sling, so those who go to battle empty-handed (weaponless) would be chided, jested, or mocked by their fellows as going to war with their two balls (testicles) to be eaten raw by the enemies. It would be "the funniest joke ever told" if a person went to the battlefield empty-handed, or without any weapon at all.

Kabaroan Eskrima, however, is simply another way of cooking the same chicken with the same ingredients, spices and all. No wonder the May 1990 issue of *Black Belt Magazine* probably saw fit to put on its front cover a brief word that Kabaroan is "The Best of Filipino Arnis."

Of course, everyone is entitled to their own perception and opinion. Kabaroan practitioners have never claimed their style or system to be better, much less the best. Certainly, the Barons' Eskrima Way is not better that its counterparts. On the contrary, we simply "Speak softly but carry a big stick." It's just quite different to wield a bigger Eskrima weapon.

But that same quote of President Theodore Roosevelt (1904) happens to be the Eskrima saying or martial arts philosophy of my father, Ramiro Abellera Estalilla Sr.

(1895-1976), who lived in America from 1921 to 1929, and taught Eskrima Kabaroan in Seattle, Washington and in Minneapolis, Minnesota. Unless there were others ahead of him, could he (Estalilla) likely be the father or grandfather of Eskrima in America? Just wondering.

SECTION II

Overview of Kabaroan Techniques

CHAPTER 4

Basic Offensive Techniques

This chapter offers an overview of the basic offensive techniques of Kabaroan Eskrima. Please refer to the Glossary of Terms in Section IV Appendices for a complete listing.

Six Types of Strikes

Within Kabaroan there are six types (kinds) of strikes:

Chop (Tadtad)—a type of strike with a downward chopping action of weapon.

Slash (Pa-Iwa)—a type of strike with a slicing action of weapon.

Thrust (Bagsul, Duyok, Tibsuk)—a type of strike with the tip or front end of weapon.

Butt (Bambu)—a type of strike with the butt end of weapon.

Gore (Suag)—a type of two-handed strike similar to a goring of a horn.

Slam (Barang)—a type of two-handed strike with the middle portion of weapon.

I use the following description so that the students can memorize the types of strikes: "Not only Chop, Slash and Thrust, Butt also Gore and Slam."

Eight Lines of Strikes

The eight lines are taken from the perpendicular, horizontal, and diagonal lines drawn from the midpoint of each side to its opposite side midpoint of an octagon. With the perpendicular line as the point or center of reference, there are three left side strikes, two main centerline strikes, and three right side strikes. From the viewpoint of a person looking at a picture or from the standpoint of the striker, and not the target or receiver, a line of strike is given a category, a name, and a definition.

There are three left side lines of strikes identified as:

Under Left (Arrabis)—an underhand diagonal strike ascending from left to right at 45 degrees across the target.

Horizontal Left (Tabas Kat)—a strike parallel to the ground level and moving from left to right.

Over Left (Sigpat)—an overhand or overhead diagonal strike descending from left to right at 45 degrees across the target.

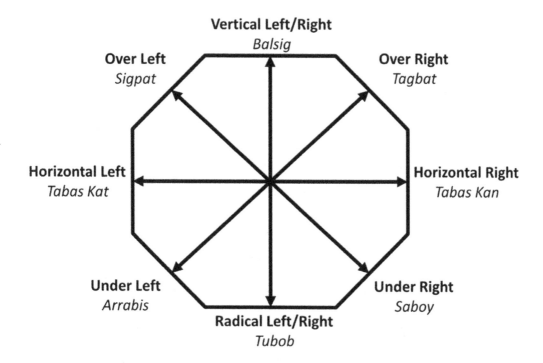

Vertical Left/Right
Balsig

Over Left
Sigpat

Over Right
Tagbat

Horizontal Left
Tabas Kat

Horizontal Right
Tabas Kan

Under Left
Arrabis

Under Right
Saboy

Radical Left/Right
Tubob

There are two centerline lines of strikes or vertical lines of strikes (Balsig), which are perpendicular overhand or overhead strike with a downward motion, from top to bottom. The two vertical strikes are designated as follows:

Vertical Left—a vertical strike executed from the left side.

Vertical Right—a vertical strike executed from the right side.

Similarly, there are two radical lines of strikes (Tubob), which are perpendicular underhand strike with an upward motion of the topside of a weapon. The two radical lines of strikes are designated as:

Radical Left—a radical strike executed from the left side.

Radical Right—a radical strike executed from the right side.

There are three right side lines of strikes identified as:

Under Right (Saboy)—an underhand diagonal strike ascending from right to left at 45 degrees across the target.

Horizontal Right (Tabas Kan)—a strike parallel to the ground level and moving from right to left.

Over Right (Tagbat)—an overhand or overhead diagonal strike descending from right to left at 45 degrees across the target.

Note that most of the six types of strikes can be executed in all eight lines of strikes. Both types and lines of strike are done at three different levels. High strikes target the head, face, neck, and shoulders; middle strikes target the chest, arms, abdomen, and waist; and low strikes target the thighs, knees, legs, and feet.

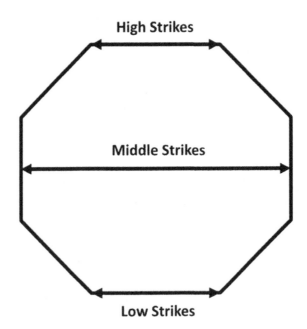

Ambidextrous Footwork

Ambidexterity is the state or quality of being able to use both hands with equal ease. The meaning is extended to apply to the feet. I believe it is advantageous, effective, and needful for an Eskrimador to be ambidextrous not only in handwork but also in footwork, even if they are said to be primarily right-handed or left-handed. One must learn the footwork that makes the left foot do what the right foot can do. Examples include Forward Step, Back Step, Forward Right Oblique, Forward Left Oblique, Backstep Right Oblique, Backstep Left Oblique, Right Sidestep, and Left Sidestep. Learn to be ambidextrous in both handwork and footwork.

There are six types of footwork employed in Kabaroan. These are:

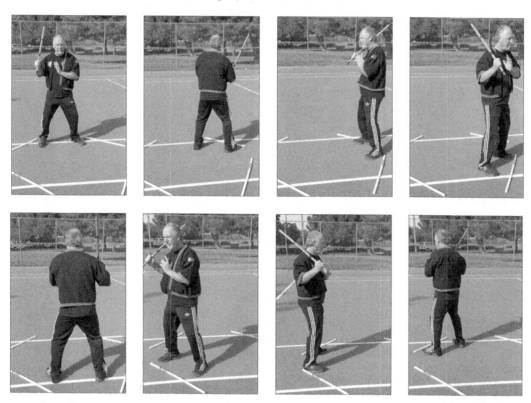

Circular (Pivotal), which follows after the lines of a circle. (inside/outside circular turns shown)

Lateral (Sideward), which tend toward the sides (front foot crossover stepping shown).

Linear (Unidirectional), going in straightforward line (forward crossover stepping shown).

Triangular, going after the shape of a triangle.

Trapezoidal, going after the shape of a trapezoid.

Multi-Directional, which tends toward many directions (not shown).

Fighting Distances and Ranges

There are three fighting ranges in Kabaroan. For simplicity and illustrative purposes, the following images show those ranges with the use of a truncheon.

Butting or Close Range—the distance at which an eskrimador can hit the opponent with the butt of his weapon; butting range. Usually this is measured by the hands ability to touch the shoulder of the opponent.

Middle or Medium Range—the distance a stick fighter can hit the opponent's body with the tip or shaft (middle) of his weapon. Usually this is measured by the practitioner touching the shoulder of the opponent with the end of the weapon.

Long or Full Range—the distance a stick fighter can hit the opponent's weapon, the extended weapon hand, or forward foot beyond the medium range. This is usually measure by the practitioner touching the extended hand of the opponent.

A practitioner with long or short weapon can execute a long-range technique, a medium-range technique, or a short-range technique. Weapons being equal, the length of weapon does not limit or prevent a martial artist from executing in any of the distances or ranges. A person with a short stick or knife can execute a Larga Mano technique, and one with a long stick can execute a Serrada (close range) technique.

It needs to be noted that, depending on the weapon of choice, the distance gap between ranges will vary greatly. The distance between long range and middle range is relatively long for a knife and the middle range and close range differential is very long for a spear. Depending on the weapons used, it is up to the practitioner to gauge their ranges by footwork and body motion.

Three ranges with knife (Close, Middle, Long):

Three ranges with spear (Close, Middle, Long):

Length of Weapon

The lengths of the various weapons used in Kabaroan are dependent on the practitioner's size. Below are the various lengths:

In order shown:

Baston—Length of figure tip to armpit

Truncheon—Length from ground to belly button

Spear—Length from ground to top of head

Bangkaw—Length from ground to chest

CHAPTER 5

Basic Defensive Techniques

Defense is defined as the act of handling an attack or offense excluding surrender; the system or method of guarding or defending against harm or danger; the way of blocking, avoiding, evading, thwarting, resisting, weakening, deflecting, suppressing, eliminating, aborting, or killing an attack. Does one evade a strike? Meet and block a strike? Merge and blend with a strike? Does one do an evasion, collision, or deflection? Surrender is considered a defeat, not a defense.

Eskrima has built-in defense techniques with and without weapons. There are two kinds of defense systems: evasion and deflection. The names of defenses are derived from the lines of strikes. Numerous are the functions of the back-up hand, which is sometimes called the empty or live (alive) hand.

In Kabaroan, there are two primary methods for defending a strike. One can meet the attack head-on with force against force, which is called the Tiradin System of Defense, or by merging or blending into the strike, which is called Todasan. These two methods can be executed from any angle of attack. These two methods of defenses are primarily executed by a single hand method called Sencillian, but may also be executed use a two-handed method called Bambolian.

There are two sides of a quarter coin: a head on one and a tail on the other. If you toss it up and it falls, does the value of the coin change if one of the sides shows up? No, the value of the coin remains. In Kabaroan, TIRADIN and TODASAN are like the two sides of the coin. Both sides are useful and helpful with their major evasion and deflection moves in both defensive and offensive situations.

Tiradin and Todasan

Tiradin (meaning strike back) is the most common or popular way of defending against a strike. Hit back, force against force, strike back. On the other hand, Todasan (meaning an all-out, to the finish, end it, finish it off, elimination, annihilation, or extermination) is the uncommon or less popular way of ending a confrontation.

Example of Tiraden (force against force) from an over-right strike

Example of Todasan (merge) from an over-right strike

Bambolia Blocks

Bambolian blocks are executed in two ways, either by Metronome blocks or by Pendulum blocks. As the names imply, Metronome blocks moves from side to side in an upward fashion, while Pendulum blocks move from side to side in a downward fashion.

Pendulum block

Metronome block

The outer line of the octagon illustrates the various angles of blocks, which are named from the perspective of the attacker. Below is a diagram with the associate block nomenclature.

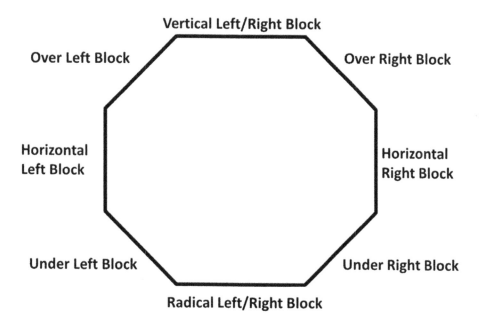

Note that the blocks are named from the perspective of the attacker. The diagram identifies the block from the defender.

CHAPTER 6

Disarming and Counter Techniques

Disarming is defined as the technique or method of removing your opponent's weapon. Trapping your opponent's hand that wields the weapon many times precedes or occurs simultaneously with the disarming. And if you counter while disarming or after disarming, what is your motive and intention? What is your purpose? During the process of disarming, you can do two things to your opponent. First, you must decide if you want to hurt your opponent while disarming him. If yes, to what degree? And second, you can decide if you want to disarm your opponent without hurting him.

Disarming and Trapping Techniques

In Kabaroan, there are general two types and three categories of disarming.

Type 1. Direct Disarms. First are direct disarms, which refer to a direct hit to the weapon in the hand, or the side of the head, that controls it. Sometimes, a direct strike to the weapon itself disarms the opponent.

Example of a Direct Disarm

Type 2. Indirect Disarms. Second are indirect disarms, which refer to a technique of a successful defense before executing a disarm. The third are empty-hand disarms, which are disarming only with the back-up hand. This presupposes that either you are unarmed (weaponless) from the start or you were disarmed by your opponent (assuming you did not disarm yourself). The empty-hand disarm also applies when at the outset you do not have any weapon at all, or when you are totally disarmed by your opponent.

Example of Empty Hand Disarm

Disclaimer: If you are completely disarmed by your equally skilled opponent, what are his chances of winning without your weapons? Or, in the reverse situation, if you have disarmed your skillful opponent, what are his chances against your skills without weapons? Do you throw away your weapons and resort to fighting without weapons? That is not the norm in battle. Find another way.

Kabaroan expands on the indirect disarm into three types: primary, secondary, and tertiary. Before executing any disarm, you must have successfully blocked your opponent's strike. The successful block creates a set of quadrants that each of the disarms are applied.

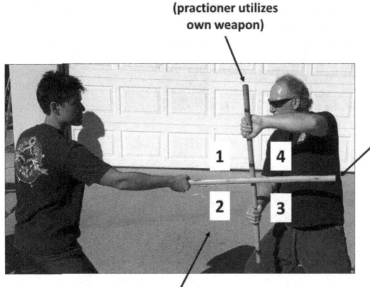

Secondary Disarms
(practioner utilizes
own weapon)

Primary Disarms
(back-up hand utilizes
opponents weapon)

Tertiary Disarms
(Back-up hand focuses
on 4 quadrants)

The primary type of disarm is executed by the use of both the weapon (baston) and the back-up hand. This is the way of using your other hand (the back-up or empty hand) against the opponent's hand or weapon to disarm, while your hand that wields or holds the weapon is doing its own work. (I prefer to call the other hand as "the back-up" rather than "alive" or "live" for the simple reason that the weapon-holding hand is equally alive and active, not dead or idle.) This type can be executed and achieved in all the three subsystems of Kabaroan.

Example of Primary Disarm

The secondary type of disarm is solely executed with the weapon hand. This is the skillful way of using your weapon to disarm your opponent, using your weapon to skillfully scoop, twist, wrench, and take away your opponent's weapon.

Example of Secondary Disarm

The tertiary type of disarm solely employs the back-up hand (or weaponless alternative). This is the third or last type of disarming, and involves disarming your opponent using only your empty hand.

Example of Tertiary Disarm

Counter Disarms

For each disarm there is a counter to that disarm, and a counter to that one, etc. Below are some examples of disarm counters:

Counter disarm from a primary disarm

Counter disarm from a secondary disarm

Counter disarm from a tertiary disarm

Counter Striking

Timing of counter strikes is critical in completing a successful defense with a course of action. There are three ways or executing these counters. The first occurs after the successful defense by the method of riposte. The method requires a follow-up by evading, meeting, or merging against any strike. In fencing, the term refers to a quick return thrust following a parry. In Kabaroan, it is the curving or serpentine movement of the weapon to avoid being hit.

Example of over-right riposte

Example of under-left riposte

Example of riposte application from under-right

Example of riposte application from under-left

Note that a riposte can be executed from any angle of attack.

The second is during the attack and called a concomitant technique, which will defend and attack at the same time.

Example of meet concomitant

Example of merge concomitant

Note that a concomitant can be executed at any angle of attack.

The third is right after the successful defense and before the next offensive attack. This must be done a fluid and quick fashion, which will come with practice. The rules of safety still apply. Below are examples of some typical Kabaroan offensive counters.

Counter strike after an over-left followed up with a over-left gore and butt strike

Counter strike after an over-right followed up with a over-right gore and butt strike

The following examples show a counter strike followed up with a concomitant lock.

Example of counter follow-up and lock for an under-left

Example of counter follow-up and lock from an over-left

The type of strike chosen for counter depends on the situation, the process of self-discovery, and the objective. Is your intent to stun, disable temporarily or permanently, or to kill the opponent? What level or degree of force should be employed? Should you employ minimum, medium, or heavy force or, on the other hand, light or deadly force? The type of strike chosen for counter depends on the preceding or previous movement executed. It must be smooth and flowing in transition; it must be economical in time and motion; and, it must be efficient, effective, and explosive.

Partners should attempt to discover all possible options in a defense by using the probing question, "What if I do this?"

CHAPTER 7

Introduction to Double Weapons

This section shows the simple (as opposed to compound or complex, and distinct from composite) method or way of doing the Eskrima Art of the Barons.

As there are many ways of killing and cooking chicken, so there are many ways of doing and practicing the Filipino martial art of Eskrima. Among them is the way the Filipino leaders called Ka (a term of respect for elders and leaders) Baroang (Baruang or Barwang).

One way of presenting Kabaroan (the term is both applicable to the person as practitioner and to the art as a style or system) is the utilization of weapons in fighting battles: long-range, medium-range, and short-range weapons.

The foregoing outline reveals the width and breadth of Eskrima Kabaroan as a system of fighting arts. Literally, it presents a cross-section of the whole spectrum of the Filipino martial arts that are weapon-based.

We could have presented first the compound (double) weaponry, instead of the simple (single) weaponry for the simple reason that, analogously speaking, people normally start learning to use both hands and feet, or both eyes and ears. If that's debatable, it's all right to disagree in a free country.

We zero in and expand on double weaponry. Regardless of the type or kind of weapon before the advent of gunpowder and the invention of firearms such as pistols, rifles, revolvers, machine-guns, bombs and cannons, the nonfirearm weapons (blunt or bladed) of any kind, type, shape, length or form may be classified under two categories: weapons of equal length and weapons of unequal lengths.

Weapons of Equal Length

Under "weapons of equal length" falls the following double weapon subclass or subsection:

1. Double Dagger or Short Batons
2. Double Batons or Short Canes
3. Double Truncheon or Pang-or
4. Double Bladed Swords or Kampilans
5. Double Bangkaw or Shield Staff
6. Double Spear or Pika/Sibat

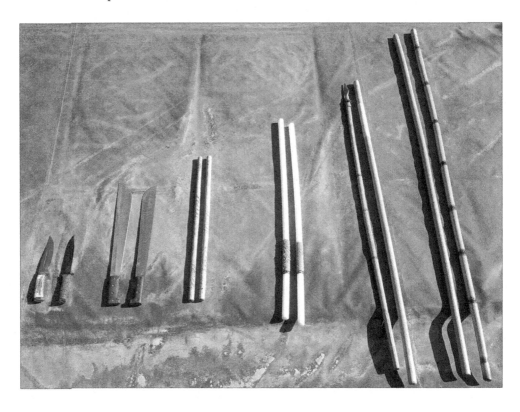

Weapons of Unequal Length

Under "weapons of unequal length" comes the following double weaponry subclass or subsection:

1. Sword and Dagger or Espada y Daga
2. Shield Staff and Truncheon or Bangkaw and Pang-or
3. Shield Staff and Spear or Bangkaw and Pika/Sibat
4. Shield and Bangkaw or Kalasag and Substitute Shield
5. Compound Weaponry for Long and Medium-Range Combats
6. Compound Weaponry for Short-Range Combats

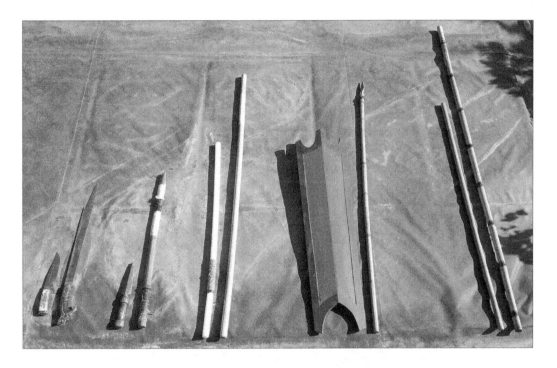

Sinawali Striking Patterns

Sinawali refers to a striking pattern with the use of two weapons, whether weapons of equal or unequal lengths. It can also be applied to the use of single weapon in Bambolia style, in contrast with Sencilia.

The Sinawali or weaving pattern of strikes is characterized by interweaving, alternating, interlacing, and/or crisscrossing right- and-left-hand held weapons, and/or high and low levels of strikes, and/or right- and left-side strikes. As long as one of these characteristics is present, it is deemed or considered Sinawali. Any two or more strikes on the same side and level by the same hand weapon are not valid as Sinawali. For example, two over-right or two over-left simultaneously with the same hand are not Sinawali patterns.

Sinawali, or weaving patterns, are derived from the intertwining and interlocking forms of sawalis (bamboo splits, forest vines, cured palm tree leaves, and other similar materials, including wires and plastics today) used for house sidings, yard fences, mats and hats, baskets, chicken cages, etc.

General Category of Sinawalis

There are three general categories of Sinawalis in Kabaroan; Binaston, which consist of using two weapons, canes or bastons of equal length, Binankaw, which involves the use of two weapons of unequal length, Bambolian or Binambolian, which consist of just one weapon such as a truncheon, a substitute shield staff, short or long staff.

The three categories equal 100 percent. Each of the three is equal to thirty-three-and-one-third percent.

Example of Binaston Sinawali category (weapons of equal length)

Example of Binankaw Sinawali category (weapons of unequal length)

Example of Bambolian Sinawali category (just one wewapon)

Observing the Rules of Safety

In order to prevent accidents and injuries, here are some rules of safety, just like safety rules in traffic and driving, occupations, sports competitions, and other activities. Follow them and you won't go wrong; disregard them and you won't go right. Observe them to maximize learning enjoyment. Avoid injuring your training and learning partner. In a cultural approach to the martial arts, you don't need to have the "animal and killer instinct."

There are three simple rules: self-control, simulation, and slow motion. First, control yourself, your attitude and state of mind, strikes and forms, exercises and defenses, offensive moves, disarms and counters. Second, simulate the likeness of a strong and powerful strike. Third, execute them in slow motion. Speed will come later. Step on the gas and develop speed gradually. No matter what the strike may be, just simulate in slow motion with self-control within your soul.

Circumspectly, observe proper distance along with the Code of Honor and Rules of Conduct for a Kabaroan practitioner or Eskrimador; you become a "Sir Baron" or "Lord Baron," a third step from the Knight in the Ladder of Nobility, according to Asian and European concepts and standards.

Weapons of Equal Lengths

BINASTON SINAWALIS (FIRST GENERAL CATEGORY)

There are seven levels of Binaston Sinawali: single, double, triple, quadruple, quintuple, hextuple, and septuple. Each level has patterns ranging from five to twenty-eight or more, and available in two-man-form executions and exercises for single or multiple-opponent situations while in defensive and offensive techniques or modes, with or without weapons (empty-handed).

For an overview, single Sinawali has fifteen (15) patterns; double has twenty-four (24) patterns; triple has twenty-eight (28) patterns; quadruple has about five (5) patterns; quintuple has five (5) patterns; hextuple has five (5) patterns; and septuple has five (5) patterns.

The important thing is to learn the principles of form (anyo or kata) formation in both single and double weaponry, and discover the rest of the forms and techniques that are available in the systems and arts. Anyway, there is nothing new under the sun, said the wise King Solomon. What one thinks is new was probably known and discovered a long time ago.

THREE MODES FOR ALL SINAWALI PATTERNS

By mode, as used here, for the impact of two weapons, we refer to the manner, way, or method of their impacts analogous to the movement of two automobiles in accidents such as rear-ending, head-on collision, sideswiping or broad-siding. What is the mode (manner) of transportation? We often get the answer as by train, boat, plane, or bus? Or by a broomstick?

What is the mode of the weapon strike? Force against force (meet-meet) is like a head-on collision of automobiles. Merging with the force is like rear-ending (merge-merge). Half-meeting and half-merging (meet-merge) with the force is like side-swiping or broad-siding. This is what we mean by mode. The three modes may be used in both single weapon and double weapon, just as you would employ the two generals— Tiradin and Todasan with their majors— evasion and deflection in both offensive and defensive situations and mobilizations as described before.

SINGLE SINAWALI UNDER DOUBLE WEAPONRY (BALANCED PATTERN)

Single Sinawali (weave) is defined or described as consisting of one strike per weapon: one on each side (right and left) of the target. The strike is executed as seen from the striker's viewpoint.

Example of Single Sinawali (balanced pattern) all-meet:

Start from a high open position

Over-right meet, under-left meet

Over-right meet, over left meet

Under-right meet; over left meet and repeat

Example of Single Sinawali (balanced pattern) meet-merge.

To introduce merging into the Sinawali, do the pattern above with someone who feeds and the other (practitioner) who does the merge. The merge is executed on the second strike (the "under" strike) by merging down onto the under strike.

Start in high open position

Over-right meet, under-left merge

Over-right meet, over-left meet

Under-right merge, over-left meet

The process of self-discovery with this pattern is that the meet or merge can be done by the practitioner with either hand or single hand and also that a strike can have three levels: high, middle, or low. In addition, both the feeder and the practitioner can strike by chopping, slicing (slashing), or thrusting. With these many variables, it is obvious that it is beyond the scope shown in this book.

DOUBLE SINAWALI UNDER DOUBLE WEAPONRY (HIGH-LOW)

Based on the definition of Single Sinawali, the definition for double and the rest of the Sinawalis, including the weapons of unequal lengths and the Bambolian Sinawali, should be easy to comprehend and execute the strikes.

Double Sinawali is defined as consisting of two strikes per weapon, alternating or crisscrossing, with a total of two strikes on each side of the target. The five most common out of twenty-four available patterns are here given as examples.

One of the most common Double Sinawali patterns is the high-low pattern. With the Eskrima octagon (lines of strike) in mind as tool of learning and teaching, do with the right hand an over-right meet, followed by a right hand under-left; next, do a left hand over-left followed by a left hand under-right meet. Now you get a total of two strikes on the right side, and two strikes on the left side.

Double Sinawali High-Low Meet-Meet pattern

What if you convert or change one strike of each weapon from a meet to a merge? You get a combination of meet and merge.

The feeder continues to feed the same pattern of high-low, but the practitioner will change from meeting the low strike to merging the low strike. As you continue to do this pattern, you begin to realize the concomitant or simultaneous defense and attack applications. Remember that this still complies with the Sinawali requirement: alternating weapons, interweaving patterns, crisscrossing, and interlacing designs.

Double Sinawali High-Low Meet-Merge

For the purpose of self-discovery, try these patterns using a single hand or alternating hands as well as changing from slash to thrust. Again, the combinations and variables are beyond this text.

Disclaimer: Sometimes, in describing Sinawali, like in arithmetic additions, a minor error is made and carried over and forwarded to the next column. Inadvertently, Double Sinawali has been wrongly called and referred to as Single Sinawali, and Triple Sinawali has been unintentionally called Double Sinawali. It's no big deal, but still we are trying to correct the little errors. By defining the terms, we hope to restore the right names and set the record straight.

TRIPLE SINAWALI UNDER DOUBLE WEAPONRY (HEAVEN AND EARTH)

Triple Sinawali is defined under Double (compuesta, compound, or composite) Weaponry as consisting of three weapon strikes on both the left and right sides. There are fourteen up to twenty-eight possible and available patterns or variations. Three of the fourteen are executed with each weapon three times and distributed in three different areas. The others are executed with alternating, interweaving, crisscrossing, and interlacing or interlocking strikes.

The first Triple Sinawali pattern is a very common pattern called Heaven and Earth; it is called this by some good Arnisadors or Eskrimadors. (I like those terms because they describe where to send your opponents or where you go if something goes wrong; in other words, their souls to heaven and their bodies to the earth.) The Sinawalis are composed of two over-right and one under-left, then transitioning to the other side with two over-lefts and one under-left. Using the Eskrima octagon, prepare to do the first patterns step-by-step by positioning both weapons beside and over the right shoulder into an open position. Weapons are about parallel to each other at 45 degrees with tips pointed toward the back. This position is called open beginning. To start the first triple weave (Heaven and Earth), do an over-right with your left weapon and then bring it under your right elbow to protect your right knee. Next, do over-right with your right weapon and then shift it over your left shoulder as you strike under-right with your left weapon and shift it to the left side and parallel to your right weapon so that both weapons are positioned just like they were on the right side, but now on the left. You just did the first half-cycle on the right side. Now do the second half-cycle on the left side exactly opposite what you did on the right side in order to complete the full cycle.

Example of Triple Sinawali Heaven and
Earth—All Meet

Practice with a partner. Remember to observe the Rules of Safety with proper distance from your partner. Strike with the correct angle or degree. Avoid hitting any part of your training partner's body, hands, head, thighs, and legs. Protect your partner. He is not your enemy.

Help prevent accidents by following the safety rules, the Code of Honor and Rules of Conduct. If you hit your partner in the temple with small sticks, they may see small stars; if you hit them with big sticks, they will see big stars, or else fall into the twilight zone. Be prudent and careful. Precaution is the first caution. Do not send them to heaven or earth.

Similar to the previous Sinawalis examples, we can introduce the meet-merge pattern. The feeder continues the pattern in the same manner as the first example, but the practitioner merges on the left side Triple Sinawali. The first three strikes start out the same, but instead of shifting to the left side strike, the practitioner keeps his weapons on the right side. Note that for over-strikes the practitioner merges from under and for the under-strike the practitioner merges from over.

Example of Triple Sinawali Heaven and
Earth—Meet Merge

If done correctly, the feeder will have difficulty maintaining the pattern and there are concomitant opportunities for the practitioner.

Once the meet-merge has become comfortable, it is time to move to full merge. Like the merges on the left side, the practitioner merges with the same opposite pattern of the feeder. The feeder must work hard to maintain the pattern and of course the practitioner must continue to be diligent about the rules of safety and conduct.

Example of Triple Sinawali Heaven and Earth—Full Merge

Example of Triple Sinawali Heaven and Earth—Full Merge *(continued)*

For the purpose of self-discovery, apply this to the twenty-eight possible patterns and include the alternate or single-hand approach and switching from slash/chop to thrusting patterns.

Sinawalis do not stop at triples. In Kabaroan, we practice Quadruple Sinawalis (four strikes per side), Quintuple Sinawalis (five strikes per side), Hextuple Sinawalis (six strikes per side) and Septuple Sinawalis (seven strikes per side). This is again an area of self-discovery for the practitioner and is beyond the scope of this introductory book.

Bambolian Sinawali (Compuesta)

The Bambolian Sinawali is the final category of Sinawali, with weapons of equal length in the Kabaroan system or style of Filipino martial arts weaponry. It is considered to be a compound (compuesta) weaponry system of weapons of equal length due to the manner in which we hold the weapon. That is due to the one-fourth-inch grip section, which facilitates two equal length sections at each end of the weapon. There are five (5) or maybe more levels and patterns of Sinawalis in Bambolian Sinawali, from singles to quadruple.

The word Bambolia or Bamboleo originates or is derived from an old Spanish verb, "bambollear" or "bambolear." It has acquired a technical and extended meaning equivalent to a strong or heavy strike—a super strike. The word "bamboozle" is likely derived from it also.

As a handed-down and passed-down term in Kabaroan, it implies a strong or super strike due to the use of both hands (either apart from or close to each other) in the execution of butt strokes, goring-thrust strikes, shaft-slam strikes, graze-jamming strikes, or defensive and offensive disarms.

The two ends and shaft of the weapon become weapons of defense and offense. In wielding, the two ends alternate and crisscross like the double batons or canes of equal and unequal lengths. There are only a limited number (about five) of Sinawalis using the chop, slash and thrust, butt, graze, gore, and slam.

Before we dive into a Sinawali, it is worth a discussion of the Bambolian technique of holding the weapon. There are two terms used for holding the weapon: one is by way of a bar-arm and the other is by way of a port-arm. The bar-arm grip is a grip where both palms face the downward position. A port-arm grip is where the palms face the opposite position. The bar-arm has only one practical option, but the port arm can either be right palm up and left palm down or vice versa.

The port-arm grip can switch freely from a right port-arm to a left port-arm by sliding the hands together, then repositioning into the opposite grip. This method of switching is called port-arm switches. The advantage to doing these switches is if you have a spear end to your weapon, port-arm switches will allow it to stay forward, which the practitioner changes for a right side stance to a left side stance.

Example of Port-Arm Switches

Much can be discovered by the practitioner of Kabaroan when it comes to Bambolian Sinawalis, but for brevity the example shows a Single Sinawali.

Example of a Bambolian Single Sinawali Balanced Pattern—All Meet

Like any Sinawali with weapons of equal lengths, the pattern can be modified.

Starting position

Over-right butt strike, under-left butt strike

Over-right butt strike, over-left butt strike

Under-right butt strike, over-right butt strike

Example of a Bambolian Single Sinawali Balanced Pattern—Meet Merge

Starting Position, over-right meet

Under-left merge, over-right meet

Over-right meet, over-left meet

Over-right merge, over-left meet, repeat

Note that these patterns and all the other Bambolian Sinawalis can be done with a butt strike or a gore strike. In addition, with either a bar-arm grip or a port-arm grip, and for that matter with port-arm switches, the practitioner can also slide one hand to the other to gain length or protect the hand. This can be done by either grip. As always, self-discovery is important in one's ability to grow as a martial artist.

Weapons of Unequal Lengths

BINANKAW SINAWALIS (SECOND GENERAL CATEGORY)

Binankaw (or binankao) Sinawali employs weapons of unequal length because one is long and the other is short. The term means involving "bankao" or "bangkaw" with another weapon.

SWORD AND DAGGER (ESPADA Y DAGA)

By far, the most common and popularly practiced style or system in this category is the Sword and Dagger technique. We like it so much, we almost left the impression that "Espada y Daga" is the only combination of the weapons of unequal length. Of course, we feel relieved that we are not alone in that situation. Many have discovered this, and among them were my teachers during the Second World War (1941-1945) in Asia and thereafter.

We are happy to pass along the information and knowledge to other students who are serious and open-minded in exploring the broad spectrum of the arts of weaponry. The other combinations have not been taught nor practiced by most styles or systems of Eskrima; they are probably less known, less common or popular, or may be unheard of at all.

Without pride or prejudice to anyone, probably only Kabaroan Eskrima practitioners teach and practice binankaw. If that is true, then we are able to offer something distinct and a little different from our peers and counterparts, and fellow lovers of martial arts. Certainly, Kabaroan is not at all better than others. It simply tries to present a cross-section and whole spectrum of the fighting weapons of the Philippines. Our ancestors employed them in their trivial warfare, tribal squabbles, and battles against foreign invaders for self and family protection; in their struggles for survival, love of country; and fighting for their faith and honor, independence, democracy, and freedom.

Earlier, we showed the various combinations offered under the weapons of unequal lengths category. In the Sword and Dagger (Espada y Daga), the dagger or punyal is used in lieu of the empty-hand, not only for parrying (deflection), locking, and blocking at close range, but also for thrusting, jamming, cutting, or disarming as a secondary weapon. It serves as the back-up weapon in instead of the empty-hand as back-up. But if the sword is lost by disarming or other means, then the dagger becomes the main or primary weapon.

If a right-handed warrior, fighter, or Eskrimador wants to hold and use the dagger as a main or primary weapon held in the right hand, that is their choice. Such is like a left-handed person with a pistol or revolver in the left hand and a sword or truncheon in the right hand. They are indeed an ambidextrous person with uncommon special abilities.

Use nonsharp plastic or rubber knives for daggers with wooden or rattan swords, symbolic of the iron or steel swords, which in turn are also symbolic of "the Sword of the Spirit" in the higher realms of life's "spiritual warfare."

Examples: Given a two-man form situation, execute in the same lines of strikes, and at the proper time for the back-up hand, use the dagger for defensive parry, block, lock, or offensive thrust and disarm. The dagger or punyal takes the place of empty-hand (often called the live hand). As a secondary weapon, like the back-up hand, the dagger is not the frontal and aggressive weapon, but the deadly treacherous back-up killer.

In the many instances of Sword and Dagger encounters, there's hardly an example of warriors in the fighting lines using the dagger as the first weapon of battle-front encounters, except in silent attack from behind enemy lines against a security guard or sentinel. If the sword is lost, the dagger becomes the main and primary weapon.

The following is an example of using the espada and the daga simultaneously. Note the concomitant attack of the espada (practiced with a baston in place of the espada).

BANGKAW (SHIELD-STAFF) AND TRUNCHEON (PANG-OR)

The bangkaw takes place as a shield and is held in the left hand in the half position. In the course of battle, a shield may become unusable; for instance a spear can impale the shield and render it awkward and useless. In this case, the shield is discarded and the bangkaw is employed, thus the reference to a "shield-staff." The truncheon (pang-or) is held in the other hand at the quarter position. The truncheon becomes the main or primary offensive weapon, while the bangkaw become a defensive weapon. It's all right if others do not see the logic of this reasoning, but would use the bangkaw as their primary or main weapon. The point is that at the onset of the battle the roles are set, but during the course of the fight, weapons interchange between offensive to defensive and visa versa.

A common exercise with the bangkaw and truncheon is a seventeen-strike fluid pattern. It begins with a ready position of bangkaw in front as a shield and the truncheon behind the bangkaw. The practitioner begins a figure eight, but this time the truncheons strikes the back end of the bangkaw to help facilitate the figure eight motion; the figure eight is completed back to ready position (strikes ten to twelve).

To get the motion started, the truncheon will strike the bangkaw with an over-left (strike one).

The bangkaw begins a figure eight pattern to the right side of the practitioner (strikes two to five).

A full figure eight is made, thus returning the practitioner to his ready position.

The truncheon now strikes the bangkaw with an upward radical strike, thus rotating the weapon upward (strikes six and seven). The truncheon again strikes the weapon with a downward vertical strike, which propels the bangkaw downward (strikes eight and nine).

The practitioner begins a figure eight, but this time the truncheons strikes the back end of the bangkaw to help facilitate the figure eight motion; the figure eight is completed, back to ready position (strikes ten to twelve).

The practitioner employs a horizontal left strike with the bangkaw to his right side (strikes thirteen and fourteen). The bangkaw is stabilized by the truncheon and the index finger of the right hand; also the bangkaw is "elongated" to the end.

(Note: "elongation" is the action of moving your hand from one position of the weapon to another by the momentum of the movement.)

From this position, execute a horizontal right with the elongated bangkaw to a downward vertical strike to the ground then thrust forward, retract the weapon back to ready position (strikes fifteen to seventeen).

There are various applications for within this pattern, as shown below.

Bangkaw and Trunchen Application 1

The opponent strikes with an over-right; the defender simultaneously blocks the attack with the bangkaw and applies a direct right strike to the hand of the opponent; the momentum of the movement continues upward, where the defender strikes the arm of the opponent with the butt of the bangkaw.

Bangkaw and Trunchen Application 2

The opponent strikes with a mid-level thrust; the defender simultaneously parries the attack with the bangkaw and applies a direct over-right strike to the hand of the opponent; the momentum of the movement continues downward, where the defender strikes the opponent's head with the butt of the bangkaw.

Bangkaw and Trunchen Application 3

The opponent strikes with an over-left slash; the defender is in the elongated position and strikes the opponent's knee with the end (or spearhead) of the bangkaw.

SHIELD-STAFF AND SPEAR (BANGKAW AND PIKA/SIBAT)

In the Shield-Staff and Spear (bangkaw and pika/sibat), the bangkaw is the secondary weapon held with the left hand. The sibat is held in the right hand, with either a throwing position or a thrusting position. Both weapons are held half-way on the weapons.

Example of the two Shield and Spear guard positions:

Thrusting position

Throwing position

The spear can be replaced with a long staff and the shield can be replaced with a bangkaw. The two positions are shown:

In order to change position, the practitioner must palm roll the sibat.

From the spear position, the spear rotates counterclockwise or forward to the thrusting position. The sibat rotation stops by striking the bangkaw, which is placed in a horizontal position.

The spear is rotated at the palm in a counterclockwise rotation.

At completion, the spearhead is facing backward. The practitioner then brings the spear down to a thrusting position:

With practice and speed, the spear can be rotated with the palm facing vertically.

The momentum of the spear can be stopped using the bangkaw.

This technique serves to keep the spearhead forward, as well as creates a distraction to the opponent. Done in sequence, it can deflect an opponent's attack while employing a deadly thrust or throw.

Another weapon manipulation essential to the spear (sibat) and bangkaw (binankaw) weapon combination is the thrust of the spear. This is achieved by a whole-body motion propelling the spear forward. It is important to practice using the whole length of the spear, as well as thrusting toward a specific target.

Example of sibat thrusting practice

Example of sibat and bangkaw thrusting application

Opponent strikes with an elongated horizontal right. Practitioner blocks the strike with a vertical butt strike with the bangkaw end and simultaneously thrusts the spear into the opponent's side.

A set of Sinawali-like patterns can be developed with the bangkaw and spear, as illustrated by this exchange.

Disclaimer: Training partners must simulate a throw or thrust of the spear and control its elongation to prevent and forestall against any possible accident. Precaution is the first caution. We don't have to prove that the weapons hurt. Some wise men have said that experience is the best teacher, and that what is self-evident needs no proof.

SECTION III

Training Exercises and Forms

CHAPTER 8

Kabaroan Multipurpose Exercises

Workout Versus Battle Exercises

Workout exercises are like battle exercises. The mock usually precedes the real. The former is a preparation for the latter. Both are real, but the one prepares for the other. Exercises are practices for real encounters. If one is to make the most of his time and develop skills with weapons to the maximum, it is best to do all exercises with weapons. To progress, exercise from light to moderate or from nonrigorous to rigorous workouts, if so desired. The purpose is to develop proficiency in weaponry and at the same time achieve the other goals of exercises—agility, stamina, power, strength, speed, form, grace, and beauty. Exercises with weapons can be done without weapons just as well.

Common Exercises

With single or double weapons, the following are some suggested exercises.

All-Thrust Exercise—from lower open position, alternate right and left thrusts.

All-Slash Exercise—from lower upper position, alternate right and left slashes.

Single Rowboat (one direction)—from upper right gore position, reach out as far as possible and bring the staff back, as though rowing a boat with single paddle.

Double Rowboat (one direction)—from upper right gore position, reach out as far as possible and bring the staff back left then right, as though rowing a boat with two paddles.

Note that all exercises have their application and modifications. Below is an example of "elongating" the weapon, as though reaching out for a strike.

Example of Single Rowboat (one direction) elongation

Example of Double Rowboat (one direction) elongation

Warning: Be aware that there are some popular exercises usually taught in schools, colleges, and universities that are no good for the Kabaroan martial artist. Many institutions and experts are discovering them, but they are very cautious and conservative in discouraging them. Find out and watch out for yourself and others you teach.

Nutrition, Recreation, and Rest

A balanced program of proper nutrition, regular exercise with wholesome recreation, and adequate and regular rest is good for a healthy body (soma), soul (psyche), and spirit (pneuma), which constitute the whole person.

We suggest that martial artists exercise temperance and prudence in what they eat, what they do for diversions and recreation, and balance their workout and practice with sufficient rest. There are many helpful books, magazines, and videotapes on the market on the subject. Let us seek the wise counsel of the experts and authorities on those subjects.

At this point, let me recall and point out the advice of the Apostle Paul to a young man named Timothy:

"But refuse profane and old wives' fables, and exercise thyself rather unto Godliness. For bodily exercise profiteth little; but Godliness is profitable unto all things, having promise of the life that now is, and of that which is to come." (I TIM. 4:7,8)

"Let no man despise thy youth; but be thou an example of the believers, in word, in conversation, in charity, in spirit, in faith, in purity." (I TIM. 4:12)

Saint Paul's ideal person and great example is Jesus Christ, who "increased in wisdom, and stature, and in favor with God and man." (Luke 2:52)

Christ's development when He was on earth in human form was four-fold and well-balanced. He increased intellectually (wisdom), physically (stature), and spiritually (favor with God), and socially (favor with man).

The persons we choose to follow and the choices we make are of tremendous importance and of eternal consequence.

CHAPTER 9

Kabaroan Eskrima Forms and Dances

One dictionary (RHWCD1997) defines the word "form" and gives thirty-eight meanings and applications. In Tagalog (the basis of the Filipino national language), the word is "anyo." In Eskrima Kabaroan, we define form as a set of strikes derived from the eight lines and six types (kinds) of possible weapon strikes by practitioners and/or protagonists.

The set of forms is a series of common, regular, and most possible strikes prearranged sequentially and consecutively in such a manner and way, movement, and method with handwork and footwork that there is fluidity and grace, economy of time, effort, and motion, and effective delivery with maximum safety.

Eskrima forms are like shadow boxing practices; with or without a partner, they are tools and aids in teaching and learning intended to develop accuracy, confidence, mobility, precision, power, proficiency, and speed, resulting in a sense of accomplishment, a feeling of completion, and satisfaction.

The letters O, P, S, T can be arranged to form five meaningful words: POST, POTS, TOPS, STOP, SPOT; or eighteen meaningless ones: OPST, OPTS, OSPT, OSTP, OTSP, OTPS, PSTO, PTSO, PTOS, PSOT, TSPO, TPSO, TOSP, TSOP, SOPT, SOTP, STPO, and SPTO.

Words are made from six vowels and twenty-one consonants in the English alphabets. From seven English music alphabets (ABCDEFG) came twelve semi-tones, chord forms, and billions of songs, melodies, and symphonies are composed! Great paintings from a few basic colors! Many forms from eight specific lines and six types (kinds) of strikes! Or from the basic three general lines of strikes: perpendicular, horizontal, and diagonal (PHD)!

Basic 12 Linear Form and Karenza

This form is a basic single-stick form (usually performed with a truncheon) that employs all of the six types of strikes and angles of attack. It can be performed as a single form or with a partner.

(Note the movement in the photos is going from right to left, though the photo steps below are to be read from left to right.)

Start at ready position, thrust, under-left slash

Over-left, step forward, under-right

Over-right, step back, vertical left, horizontal left gore:

Step forward (horse stance), horizontal right gore, under-right gore

Over-right gore, step forward with over-right butt, step forward with over-left butt

Turn and repeat

The Basic 12 is fundamental to understanding and practicing the six types of strike, Sencillian versus Bambolian and lines of strikes. They can also be employed as two-man forms. The following are Sencillian two-man forms taken from the cadenza.

Example of Tiraden defense:

For safety, the two participates measure their distance. The feeder (left) thrusts defender (right) merges

Feeder executes under-left slash; defender meets attack

Feeder executes over-left slash; defender meets attack

Feeder steps forward and executes under-right slash; defender steps back and meets attack

Feeder executes over-right slash; defender meets attack

Feeder steps back and executes vertical left slash; defender merges attack. From this position the roles change and the defender becomes the feeder and executes a thrust. This is a continuous pattern, changing from offense to defense.

Example of Todasan defense:

 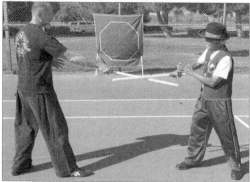

The feeder (left) thrust defender (right) merges

Feeder executes under-left slash; defender merges attack

Feeder executes over-left slash; defender merges attack

Feeder steps forward and executes under-right slash; defender merges attack

Feeder executes over-right slash; defender merges attack

Feeder steps back and executes vertical left slash; defender merges attack. From this position the roles change and the defender becomes the feeder and executes a thrust. This is a continuous pattern, changing from offense to defense.

These examples can change from meeting to merging movement. For the purpose of self-discovery, I encourage the participants to become comfortable with this form and change the approach from meeting to merging, from linear movement to circular movement, and from thrust to slashes.

Note that the Bambolian portion is not shown due to brevity, but from the previous discussion the practitioners can practice and evolve this form.

General Tiradin form Karenza

From ready position, middle thrust, over-left slash, step forward over-right slash, step forward horizontal left slash.

Horizontal right slash, catch, step forward metronome block to the right, step forward, pendulum block to the left, under-left slash, step back and under-right slash.

Catch in right side roof block, over-right slash, catch, metronome block to right side, pendulum block to left side, roof block to left side.

Step forward and under-right slash, turn 180 degrees by stepping back with right foot and execute an over-right slash, vertical left to the ground, back to ready and repeat in opposite direction.

Like the Basic 12, general Tiradin can also be performed as a two-man form. This is something that can be self-discovered and beyond the scope of this book.

Basic Bambolia 11

The Bambolian 11 addresses all the Bambolian types of strikes and lines of strikes.

Starting prayer, step right foot forward, over-right butt strike, step forward over-left butt strike, horizontal right butt strike, vertical left butt

Radical right butt strike, horizontal left butt strike

Vertical right butt strike, radical left butt strike, step forward with under-right butt strike

Step forward with under-left butt strike, step forward, horizontal slam

For each of these forms, there are variations, which for brevity are in not in this book. Think of symmetry, footwork and application and these forms can be continually expanded and developed.

For weaponless or empty-hand forms, whether in single or double weapon classification, the term Kabarachi (the last two syllables being adopted) has been used since 1976 in Fresno, California. They take on the same movements, but in a continuous slow movement. Due to the various angles and movements, Kabarachi can be practiced and is beneficial throughout one's life.

CHAPTER 10

The Legacy of Ramiro Abellera Estalilla Sr.

An art will die unless you practice and teach it. That was the reason why my father, Ramiro Abellera Estalilla Sr. (1895-1976) began teaching Kabaroan (also known as Panagigam, meaning weaponry, and Dalan ti Armas, meaning the way of weapon) in the 1920s during his early twenties. Today, it is popularly known as Eskrima, Kali, and Arnis. He propagated his art by teaching it and living it with his moral philosophy of life.

By teaching, practicing and propagating the Kabaroan fighting art and defense system of my father, I feel that I am honoring him and continue to remember him and his teacher. My father was a protégé and special student of Kabaroan Don Mariano Rigonan, who was a master swordsman or Eskrimador. I also learned the art first-hand from my father and from one of his graduate students, Uncle Bernardo U. Banay, my mother's older first cousin.

The Preparation to Inherit Kabaroan

Although a preacher by profession, I have been a practitioner of Kabaroan/Bambolia of the Rigonan-Estalilla School since I began studying it in 1946, not to mention the years of training beginning in 1941 during World War II. And today, I feel like being only a practitioner of this system, notwithstanding the black belt degree level that I hold in the Eskrima system of the Filipino Martial Arts Academy in Manila, Philippines. That being the case, and on that premise, I would probably be the only exponent, or among the few highest-ranking exponents and Kabaroans living on this North American continent.

I have been a minister since 1950 and was ordained in 1971. I attended the Manila Bible Seminary and am a graduate in theology from Philippine Bible College in Baguio City. I also studied at the Baptist Bible Seminary and taught at the Central Bible Institute in Manila. For secular education, I attended Baguio Colleges, Far Eastern University in Manila, and California State University, Fresno.

As a preacher, I attained religious convictions and spiritual education that have heavily influenced my philosophy, teaching, and practice of the Kabaroan martial art with respect to the value, sacredness, and preservation of human life.

The Early Years

My interest in Estoque (or Estocada as it is called in Nueva Ecija) began in 1936 at the age of six. This was heightened by the need for hometown, barrio, and family defense during the World War II years, 1941-1945. My systematic and serious studies began in 1946 under my Uncle Bernardo in Pagadian, Zamboanga. At first, my father was not convinced to teach me. "If you want to learn Dalan ti Armas, go to your uncle and study first with him," he said. So I went, and then two years after I studied at the Manila Bible Seminary, I visited our home in Gayonga, Cotabato, Mindanao, and began my formal studies and training with my father. Only then was my father willing to teach me the martial art of Kabaroan.

The finer points and techniques reserved by my father for himself were personally passed on to me only when I had proven and shown myself worthy to inherit them by learning the art, and proved not likely to misuse it, nor to bring disgrace and dishonor upon my father's fame and good name.

The Inheritance of Elder Ramiro

My father lived for eighty-one years (March 13, 1895-June 19, 1976). He descended from a family of Eskrimadors, or swordsmen. His grandfather, Major Eusebio Estalilla, who adopted him as an orphan, was the sparring partner of fencing master and swordsman General Antonio Luna of the Philippine Revolution against Spain.

Upon the death of "Apo" Eusebio, with General Luna in an ambush ordered by another general, Bishop Gregorio Aglipay (also a revolutionary and founder of the Philippine Independent Church) took my father, his godson, for armas de mano training. As compadre (coparent) of Eusebio and godfather of my father, Bishop Aglipay himself undertook the responsibility of teaching Eskrima to his godson. Later, he sent my father to train directly under master Eskrimador and Kabaroan Don Mariano Rigonan, who had traveled extensively to Asia and Europe.

In the 1920s, my father left to reside in the United States. As a sergeant and veteran of World War I, under some benefits he pursued studies in law and military science and tactics at Saint Thomas College in St. Paul, Minnesota. While in Minneapolis, he practiced and publicly taught Kabaroan at the Minneapolis Athletic Club. He also taught the martial art when he lived in Seattle, Washington. Among his former students in America were Bishop Dr. Enrique Sobrepena, DD; Dr. Didimo Fombuena, DD; and "Father Pono," a religious priest in Seattle, Washington.

The Great Variety of Exposures

In 1929, my father returned to the Philippines. He married Aurelia Q. Umipig, and I was born on January 23, 1930. My father organized Eskrima schools in various towns and provinces of Luzon until 1936. Those years widely exposed him to the systems and teachings of Eskrimadors Bergonia, Maglaya, Toledo, and various teachers and masters of Estocada in the northern part of the Philippines.

After serving as general campaign spokesman for Manuel Alzate (Philippine Congress), my father and his family (my mother, my younger sister Norma, and myself) migrated to Mindanao, southern Philippines, in 1936. While employed with Compania Maritima, and later with Mindanao Motor Lines, my father continued to teach his art.

Then World War II broke out. After General Douglas MacArthur left Australia for the United States, my father, who came out of the disbanded Philippine Army, became one of the founders of the People's Revolutionary Army (PRA) during the early resistance movement and guerrilla warfare in Mindanao. As one of the founders, he held the rank of a colonel until the reorganization, recognition, and merging of the United States Forces in the Philippines (USFIP) with the United States Armed Forces in the Far East (USAFFE) Divisions associated with Colonels Bowler, Fertig, and Phillip Hedge of Bukidnon and Cotabato in Mindanao.

As an Army Second Lieutenant, USFIP, my father was an Intelligence (G-2) and Executive Officer involved in the training of Bolo Battalions. As Provost Marshal, he was heavily exposed to the different Luzonian, Visayan, and Maguindanao systems of armas de mano and martial arts.

My father was adopted as an honorary son of a datu (tribal king or chief), Datu Dilanggalang of Cotabato. Because of that, he had a good access to inner circles and became very familiar with the Muslim (Maranao, Jolojano, and Maguindanao) weapon methods and fighting arts, thus enriching his arsenal of weaponry and Eskrima heritage.

Some Incidents in the Elder Ramiro's Life

Although my father was an idealist, he was also a practical man. And his philosophy was to use his Eskrima skills in the service and for the defense of his country, family, women, the defenseless, and lastly, himself. He wanted to be known as a gentleman and as chivalrous. Twice he served his country under two world wars. He was a Regimental Supply Sergeant of a branch under the California National Guard during World War I (1914-1919).

He was a First Lieutenant (one rank higher after an honorable discharge) during World War II (1941-1945). He served as Barrio Captain of Gayonga, Cotabato for twenty years (1946-1966), and as Deputy Governor of Cotabato under Governor Datu Duma or Mama Sinsuat, and/or Governor Datu Udtog Matalam within those twenty-five years after the war.

During his lifetime, there were several interesting incidents that tied his Eskrima skills with his moral philosophy of non-belligerence, and outlook on life. I have many of them, but here's the gist of some human interest stories and they are true. My memory fails me as to some names, which if I can recall I would only give the first or last names. The events are not chronological order.

In Cotabato, Mindanao, sometime between 1946-50, he broke up and locked in his arms two policemen who were fighting in Midsayap's public market over a beautiful woman employed as a beautician in my mother's beauty shop.

In 1931-32, he accepted the challenge of a travelling merchant, Sunga, who staked all of his clothing merchandise to anyone who could disarm him of his fighting baton made of palm wood. Having come from the United States, my father didn't care for the clothing. After disarming without hurting his opponent, he only asked for the baton as his trophy. He got it, and still his opponent became his friend.

In 1932-33, he pursued on horseback and rescued an elementary school teacher kidnapped and abducted by a prospective suitor who pretended to enroll his yet-unborn child, for which he was looking for a mother-to-be. The rescued woman married many years later and had a son who became a very active student leader at the University of the Philippines.

In 1929-30, a well-known boxer in the town of Munoz and rival suitor over my mother repeatedly insulted Ilocano ladies in order to provoke Ramiro Sr. to fight. Unable to draw away Ramiro Sr. from his yardwork cutting weeds with a dull weeding bolo, the boxer approached him and flung a flurry of jabs. The weeding bolo was dull, but made cuts all over his arms. The boxer filed no case when the policemen arrived and found out the whole story, which was witnessed by several women. The police officers arrested the boxer and booked him for creating disturbance.

In 1933-34, Celin climbed up the stage stopped the program during the town fiesta of Munoz, and with his cane he cautioned anyone who would try to force him leave the platform, until somebody would accept his challenge to show their Estocada greatness. That included the policemen, provided they would take off their guns and uniforms. Police Chief Dar sent for Ramiro and fetched him from across the town, without telling him the purpose. Ramiro, who was the Eskrima teacher for the whole town's police force, was prevailed upon, and out of courtesy for the police department and the town, he served. In 1970, about thirty-five years later, at age seventy-five, Ramiro made a courtesy visit to the man whom he did not intend to hurt during that fateful day, which blinded the man in the left eye. Celin, now partly senile and over eighty, had forgotten how he lost his sight. Father felt a little better, as he felt remorse during all those years because they were supposed to be friends. Was he coaxed or bribed to fight Ramiro? Nobody knows, but they remained friends.

Sometime in 1932-33, Alfonso and his brother-in-law had a disagreement that resulted in their cursing each other's mothers. Their verbal tongue-lashing over cups of sugarcane wine went beyond losing their tempers into drawing their talunasan (long bolos). Relatives and neighbors could not stop them. People in the house jumped through the windows and some fell down the bamboo stairs as they scampered to safety. Someone sent for Ramiro, who lived in the same barrio of the town. When father arrived, he told them to stop. The fighting brothers-in-law were slowing down—tired, exhausted, and unable to kill or hit each other. They pointed their weapons at each other as they said to father, "I could have killed him; I could not even hit!" Father responded that their training together under him was not for that purpose. "You are brothers and my students. You are to defend each other, not kill."

In 1941, a dozen of barrio leaders actively taught Panagigam or Armasan (as they called armas de mano in Gayonga, Cotabato), to be prepared against raids by bandits and enemy attacks. All interested youngsters and adults who wanted to defend their barrios, their families, and themselves came for an organized afternoon and evening study of techniques.

The general unwritten theme was "How Would You Defend Against This Strike?" There was Marcelino Bermudez, Lauro Cabarrubias, Menardo Presas, Braulio Roque—all from Zambales in Luzon, and Attorney Felino Abalos and my father from La Union.

One day, Braulio Roque showed what he thought was a superb and impenetrable defense by doing a redonda payong (umbrella). It is achieved by twirling the baston so fast that no rocks thrown at him would go through, or so he claimed. "How would you come up against that?" Roque asked and pressed for answer. Several tried some techniques, but they didn't work.

Father believed that for every technique, there must be a counter to it. Roque finally turned to my father and insisted that he show one technique. Father demonstrated several techniques, each of which sent Roque's baston hurling about five meters away. "That works, compadre." Roque exclaimed, as he wondered how father did it.

There were many stories related to me after my parents embraced the Christian faith, and my father was already a Bible teacher and a preacher in his own way. Some stories were told to me by other people who personally knew my father. Father was said to be a fast runner. One of his favorite games for speed and sports with his fellow youngsters was to run after a horse and catch its tail. My father also considered himself an "atheist" before World War II. After he came back alive from war, however, I heard him say many times to me (and to others); "Son, I found out that there are no atheists in the foxholes."

The Later Years of the Elder Estalilla

In 1965, my parents' return to Luzon greatly benefited me in my training. Later, in 1975, he shared his expertise and art freely with the students and teachers of the Filipino Martial Arts Academy, and the Filipino Arnis Association, of which I was a member of the Board of Directors, in Manila. The Academy's students and staff visited him freely at my home in Valenzuela, Bulacan, Metro Manila.

Father gave the finishing touches and final Kabaroan techniques to me until my forty-sixth birthday on January 23, 1976. In February, I left for the United States on a Gospel-related mission. Five months later, my father passed away, at the age of eighty-one, to meet his maker, God, whom he loved and served in the Church of Christ during the last thirty years of his life.

In all modesty, I would venture to say that father and I had two things in common: both of us are Gospel-of-love preachers and Eskrima-Arnis lovers. We have often wondered whether those qualities amalgamated and blended to make the Kabaroan art a dynamic system worth learning and passing on.

CHAPTER 11

About the Author

Ramiro U. Estalilla Jr. is a minister by profession, having graduated from the Manila Bible Seminary in 1951; the Philippine Bible College in 1953; and was first ordained in 1946 in Cotabato, Mindanao and again in 1971. He started studying Eskrima in 1941 during World War II, and began compiling notes in 1946 for an Eskrima handbook. He migrated to America as a preacher in 1976, and instituted and taught Eskrima at Fresno City College in 1982-1984 and at California State University, Fresno, with the rank of Assistant Professor, since 1990.

He founded the United States Eskrimadors Legion, the Eskrima Consultants Association, the Kabaroan Instructors Association, and The Order of Kabaroan. He has taught under the business names of Kabaroan of America, Filipino Interstyle Eskrima, and Portable State University. He was a radio broadcaster for twelve years, has taught philosophy and languages, and has been a practitioner of Eskrima since 1941.

He advocates and practices Magnetic and Scalar Energy medicine for health and healing.

He is married to Flordeliza Pastor and they have three living children, Prince, Alpha, and Brenda, as well as six living grandchildren: Karen Marie Estalilla; Sean Paige Estalilla; Courtney, Samantha and Shelby Domingo; and Nathaniel Fasching, and one great-grandson, Jace Donovan Estalilla. They have lived in Fresno since 1976. He was on the staff of the California State University since 1985, where he has taught Bible to faculty and staff, as well as sports fencing, Eskrima fitness and self-defense. He retired from Fresno State in 1996. He was inducted into the World Martial Arts Hall of Fame in 1995, 1996, and in 1999 as the world's first Filipino Doctor of Martial Arts.

After thirty-three years, Ramiro and Flor became United States citizens on July 21, 2008, when he adopted additional names. His full legal name is Silverngold Ramiro Estalilla Destiny Speaker for a special, good reason: he has written religious articles, books, songs, and music—patriotic, country, love, folk, and religious/spiritual songs.

Some Final Thoughts

Relations between Kabaroan with other systems of martial arts are compatible and complimentary. Kabaroan is compatible with and complementary to other fighting arts. It compliments and is complemented by other systems in many principles, applications, and objectives.

The moral lesson here is that we all drink water from the same source and we breath the same air. In God the Creator, we live and move and have our one life to live. May we learn to love one another and live in peace with each other. Let's master our chosen martial arts, but follow the Master of Heaven and Earth, Jesus Christ.

Notes from the Editor

I met Grand Master Ramiro Estalilla Jr. in 1994 and immediately began training with him. I was blessed to find exactly what I was looking for in a teacher. Grand Master Ramiro Estalilla Jr., whom we affectionately call "Apo," became my mentor in learning and studying martial arts, how I teach martial arts to my students, and how I should conduct myself. At the same time, he became the preverbal "wise sage" whose spiritual guidance is immeasurable to my own spiritual life. Anyone who spends any time with the man will immediately sense his genuine affection and care for their well-being, and ultimately for their walk with God.

I began to have discussions with Apo about his manuscript many years ago. In a real sense, his documentation of Kabaroan started in the 1980s, when he started teaching at Fresno State. But what is most remarkable is his dedication for the art over his entire life. There is a true authenticity to his love of Kabaroan, which stems from his love of family and respect for his teachers, in particular his father and uncle. This book is a testament to that love and dedication.

In the effort to edit this book, it was essential to keep Apo's exact words and for the reader to sense that he is talking directly to them. I only added comments and additional explanations to fully describe the techniques and some very minor grammatical corrections. Overall it is extremely important to hear Apo's voice and hear, between the words, the deeper meaning of the Kabaroan philosophy and way of life.

I would like to thank all Associate Grand Masters who helped me in this book, as well as the friends of Kabaroan (for which there are many) and to my students, whose dedication to the art of Escrima has always given energy to my true love of Filipino martial arts. I would like to thank Guro Dan Inosanto for providing us with his thoughtful foreword and Mark Wiley, who has helped me edit and produce Apo's book. Finally, of course, is the long and untiring support of my wife Nancy; she has allowed me to follow my passion with support and unconditional love.

Salamat Po,
Associate Grandmaster Guro Ron Reekers

Friends of Kabaroan

Lino Espejo (AGM)

Steve Pertzolt (AGM)

Lino Espejo (AGM), David Brandon (AGM), Mark "Crafty Dog" Denny, Ed Planas (ASM),
Gerald Beardsley (AGM)

Tim Evans Parker (AGM)

Wade Williams (AGM) with
son Keenan Williams

Robert A. White (AGM)

Ron Reekers (AGM) and
Jay Gilmore (Master)

Richard Pascual (AGM)

Master Dwight Hope

Huntington Beach Seminar 2014
(Front left to right): Steve Petzolt, Ed Almaguer, Jiame Vistacion, Ron Reekers
(Back left to right): Pat Tagudar Jr., Dr. John Hsu, Jason Nichol, Manny Mabunga, Jay
Gilmore, Chris Mabunga, Jerry Bada, Pat Tagudar III

Ed Bansuela (AGM)

Anthony Manasala (AGM)

Greg Ranin (Master)

Chris Callahan (Bachelor)

Philip Oyog (Bachelor)

Kimberly Israel and Sifu Matt Emery

Lara Wallace and Xan Wallace

Angelica Kessler

Russell Chow

Chris and CJ. Chris Jr. Nalley

Brian Cunnings (AGM)

Michael and Lizelle Hufana

PG Myrlino Hufana (AGM), GM Conrad Manaois and AG Pambuan

Matt Smith (AGM)

SECTION IV

Appendixes

APPENDIX A

Glossary of Terms

Abridged: shortened.

Adalannac: teach me.

Attack (Offense): the act of aggression, of attacking or assaulting; an aggressive movement or action designed to strike, hit, harm, or hurt an opponent.

Ambidextrous: able to do with both the left or right hand.

Anyo: form, kata.

Backhand: the strike from the other side of the body by the hand wielding the weapon.

Back-up Hand: the live, empty, weaponless hand that assists and interplays with the main hand that holds the weapon.

Bambolia: (from Spanish word "bambolear") a strike or defense executed with both hands; a two-handed super strike such as butts, gores, and slams.

Bangkao and Baston: shield staff and baton.

Bangkao and Pika: shield staff and spear.

Barang: a blocking or barring strike or defense; slam.

Baroang (Baruang, Barwang, Baruwang): Baron, Barron.

Baston: baton, stick, cane, olisi.

Compuesta (compuesto): composite, compound; two-handed double weapon subsystem.

Counter: a strike before, after, or during a defense.

Cut Over: a disengage, as in fencing, executed **over** the adversary's foil, followed immediately by a lunge or thrust.

Cut Under: a disengage, as in fencing, executed **under** the adversary's foil, followed immediately by a lunge or thrust.

Defense: the act or power of defending or guarding against an attack, harm, or danger; the act of blocking, avoiding, evading, thwarting, eliminating, aborting, or killing an attack; the act of handling an attack or offense, excluding surrender.

Defense Octagon: a defense chart based on a polygon with eight equal sides.

Deflection (Parry): a type of defense by parrying; to parry means to deflect, divert, redirect, weaken, or stop a strike or blow either by one-handed weapon parry, two-handed weapon parry, or double-weapon (composite, compound) parry.

Disarm: to remove the weapon from.

Espada y Daga: sword and dagger.

Evasion: a type of defense by evading or avoiding a strike or blow either by retreating, forward advance, oblique retreat, oblique forward advance, side stepping, ducking under high strikes, jumping over low strikes, or by simply running way.

Forehand: With the right hand, it is an UR, HR, OR, VR strike; with the left hand, it is an UL, HL, OL, and VL strike.

Intercept: to stop a hit.

Kampilan: cutlass, sword.

Karenza: martial art dance.

Latigo (Latico): whip, a type of strike after the wielding of a whip.

Lunge: thrust.

Metronum (metronome): A type (kind) of strike or defense movement that is an inversion or opposite of pendulum, with the base as pivot point; a movement derived from an instrument designed to mark exact time by a regularly repeated tick; metronum is used for rhyme and euphony.

Overhand (Overhead): Performed with the hand raised above the elbow or the arm above the shoulder. (Used interchangeably and synonymously with overhead.)

Overhead (Overhand): Above the level of the head; used in the same sense as overhand. (Used interchangeably and synonymously with overhand.)

Paayon: Merge, blend.

Pasabat: Meet, block.

Pendulum: a type (kind) of strike or defense movement with the top as pivot point and used as the opposite or inversion of metronum for instruction purpose.

Pronation (Pronine): palm of the hand facing downward or inward.

Riposte: a counterstrike after or during a successful defense or parry.

Salamat Po: thank you.

Sencilla (from Spanish word "sencillar," meaning simple or single): a strike or defense executed with single hand or weapon such as chops, slashes, and thrusts.

Strike: one of the actions or movements designed as an attack taken from any of the six types or kinds of strikes, and executed from any of the eight lines of strikes, or a combination thereof.

Supination (supine): palm of the hand facing outward or upward.

Tiradin: see chapter 2.

Todasan: see chapter 2.

Turuan Po: teach me; I am ready to learn.

Underhand (UL, UR. RL, RR): a strike done with the hand below the level of the elbow or shoulder.

Yarika: You're done, taken, finished; gotcha.

TERMS USED IN DISARMING WITH COUNTER

Alipugpug (Whirlwind): a type of defense with counter and disarm like a whirlwind.

Apegado (Apegar): at risk, risky, dangerous.

Apritar: to tighten.

Arrebato: surprise, sudden, unexpected kind of Bambolia defense with disarm and referred to as a hurricane.

Golpe (Golpear): a sudden, heavy strike associated with the expression "maso de golpe."

Kaus (Scoop, Bind): a technique that disarms with a scoop and binds the opponent's hand or weapon.

Lock/Unlock: bind/release.

Machar (Machacar): to teach a hard lesson.

Pakurus: x-block.

Ragadi: saw, sawing.

Raspar (File): a kind of strike with a filing action or method.

Raspingki: a kind of disarming technique sometimes called wrench.

Remache: a fast and direct kind of defense with disarm sometimes called blitz.

Tachar: to give a hard lesson.

Tagudan (to bruise): similar to raspar.

ADDITIONAL COMMON TERMS

Armasan: deal, go, provide, or fight with weapon.

Awan-Igam: weaponless, empty-hand.

Bakbakan: serious fight or battle.

Balila: wooden sword with eight edges and made from the bark of Philippine palm tree.

Balisong: butterfly knife; originally called Batangas knife.

Bastonan: deal, go, provide, or fight with baton or cane.

Buntalan: boxing, fisticuff.

Danza: dance.

Garrote-An: deal, go, provide, or fight with garrote or baton.

Gubatan: battlefield; battle or firing line.

Gubator (-ar): warrior.

Gunting: scissors.

Intercept: to stop a hit.

Kampilan: cutlass, sword.

Karenza: martial art dance.

Kartib: scissors.

Kaus: scoop.

Kilawen: eaten raw; figuratively, to take it easy.

Latigo (Latico): whip, horsewhip; a type of strike after the wielding of a whip.

Lateral (Parallel or Reciprocal) Hands: the right versus left, or the left versus right.

Naalaca: got you, you're mine, gotcha; same as yarika.

Pakal (Bagsul, Bagkong): ice-pick method of stabbing with, holding or wielding a knife or dagger.

Panagigam: way, method, or defense with weapon.

Pinnang-Oran: fighting with bastons or canes.

Pasikat: rising to fame (if accented on the ultima); show-off (if accented on the penult); the acronym for Philippine Amerasian systems integrating Kabaroan armas de mano training.

Saksak (Duyok, Tibsuk): bolo-hold or hammer-hold method of wielding a knife or dagger.

Sikaran: kicking fight or game.

Sipaan: kicking game Sipaan, Sikaran, Tadyakan.

Suntukan: boxing, fisticuff.

Tadek: a form of dance footwork.

Tadyakan: kick or foot fighting (more serious than sikaran).

Tagaan (Tinnagbatan): a fight with bladed weapons.

Transversal (Diagonal) Hands: the right versus right, and the left versus left.

APPENDIX B

List of Striking Techniques

Abanico Corto: a short fanning-motion type of strike or defense.

Abanico Largo: a long fanning-motion type of strike or defense.

Ascending Diagonal: under-left and under-right; a diagonal strike going up at 45 degrees from left to right, or from right to left and across the target.

Bambolia: a system of strike or defense with weapons held with both hands, usually close to or apart from each other.

Bambolian Fort-Arm: a way of holding a weapon similar to that of a rifle held in front of and diagonal to the chest and body.

Bambolian Whip: a Bambolian way of executing a whip-like snappy strike.

Bambolian Tagud: a Bambolian way of executing a heavy scratching line on the face or body parts with the front end or butt end of one's weapon.

Bambolian Triplet: a Bambolian way of executing three consecutive and successive strikes that flow and are close to each other.

Butting: a Sencillan or Bambolian strike with the either butt end of a baton or weapon.

Cerrada (Serrada): closed; a close-quarter style or system of fighting techniques associated with lighter, shorter, and smaller weapons for mobility and extra speed.

Chopping: a kind of strike such as over-left, vertical, and over-right.

Circular/Curve/Serpentine/Spiral: nonlinear strikes.

Coiling and Recoiling: a type of spiro-circular strike.

Descending Diagonal: over-right and over-left; a diagonal strike going down at 45 degrees from right to left or from left to right, and across the target.

Fanning: abanico largo (long), and abanico corto (short) strike or defense either from side to side, or from back to front.

Feinting (Faking, Lansi, Huwad): a pretend strike intended to fool or deceived.

Figura Ocho (Figure Eight): a striking motion similar to the writing of the figure or number eight (8).

Port-Arm Butt (Bambolian): a two-handed method of holding a wooden weapon, similar to the holding of a rifle with both hands under a fort-arm command.

Goring: similar to the gore action of a horned beast.

Guillotine: a disarming technique of the hand or weapon similar to the falling of an ax used to cut off heads during public execution.

Half-Beat and Off-Beat: small e; name-that-tune.

Hooking: a scooping action with the butt portion of a cane or baton.

Horizontal: a movement parallel to the ground level.

Kaus (Scoop): a hooking action with the weapon or with the hand.

Kruzado/Kruzada: a crisscrossing type or style of strike and defense with double weapon.

Latigo (Saplit, Witik): a snapping, whipping, cracking method of strike.

Metronum (Metronome): derived from the movement of an instrument designed to mark exact time by a regularly repeated tick; a movement from side to side in a metronome fashion with the base as a pivot and used as the opposite or inverse of pendulum.

Payong: umbrella; a defense method or technique derived from the use of an umbrella.

Pendulum: from side to side in a pendulum fashion, with the top as a pivot and used as the opposite or inverse of metronum.

Radical: a Kabaroan strike or defense originating from below and moving upward.

Rebounding: a bouncing action of a baton from the ground floor.

Redonda: circular, umbrella, payong.

Retracted: withdrawn.

Rompida: to tear down with successive vertical and radical, up and down strike.

Ropilon: circular, umbrella, payong.

Scooping: kaus.

Shortened: a form of retraction.

Sinawali: a weaving pattern of striking with double weapon.

Slamming: a two-handed Bambolian strike with the middle portion of a baton or cane.

Slashing/Slicing: a striking action derived from or patterned after the slicing action in the use of a knife as when cutting meat, fruits, or vegetables.

Spiral/ Serpentine/Circular/Curve: all nonlinear and non-straightforward type or kind of strike.

Tapado (Cerrado, Serrado): covered; sealed; a strike or defense that covers the opponent's line of offense; also, a style or system of Eskrima that purports to cover all lines of strikes with only three lines of strikes or defenses.

Thrusting: a straightforward striking action with the front end portion of a weapon.

Twirling: a fancy way of making a circular strike with a baton or any weapon.

Twisting: wrenching or forcibly turning from one side to another side, such as in disarming or in exercise.

Umbrella: a circular article made of cloth, paper, and wood or metal braces used for protection against the rain (paragua) or sun (parasol); a striking or defense technique derived from the use of an umbrella as covering and protecting the head or body.

Vertical: perpendicular; a strike, or line of strike or defense, derived from a 90-degree line from to bottom; a strike or defense originating from the top that is the opposite of radical.

Whipping: latigo.

Zapping: taking away, removing, depleting, consuming.

APPENDIX C

Weapons of Kabaroan

Badang: a short (12" to 16 ") and heavy single-edged bolo for cutting meat or wood.

Balila: a long (30" to 38") multi-edged (2 to 8) fighting weapon made of hard palm tree bark.

Balisong: butterfly knife also known as the Batangas knife.

Bangkao, Bangkaw, Bangkaw: shield staff.

Chakong: nunchaku.

Daga: dagger.

Gayang (Pika): spear, hunting staff.

Gulok: bolo.

Kalasag: shield.

Kampilan: cutlass sword.

Kumpay: scythe, sickle.

Kris: a two-edged wavy dagger or sword.

Pana: the arrow of a bow.

Panabas: a long-handled bladed weapon for cutting grasses and reeds.

Pang-Or: a big stick.

Punyal: dagger.

Salbatana: blow gun.

Sarukod: walking cane, or walking staff.

Talunasan: a long single-edged fighting bolo; also used of a fighting stick called balila.

Yoyo: a toy that used to be a Filipino fighting weapon; a Duncan yoyo.

APPENDIX D

Some Geometric Terms

Angle: the figure made by two intersecting straight lines.

Angular: bearing the quality of an angle.

Arc: portion of a circle.

Circular: pertaining to or following the line of a circle.

Curve: portion of a circle.

Degree: the opening or extent of an angle.

Diagonal: pertaining to the line opposite a right angle; hypotenuse.

Horizontal: pertaining to a line parallel to the ground or floor.

Hypotenuse: the straight line connecting two points from the nonintersecting sides of a right triangle; diagonal line.

Lateral: side to side; the left against the right hand of players facing each other.

Level: a point of height, position, or degree on a vertical reference or standard.

Linear: in a straight line.

Leverage: advantage, power, effectiveness.

Octagon: a polygon with eight equal sides.

Parallel: pertaining to a position of a line with another where their ends do not meet or intersect.

Perpendicular: vertical.

Radical: an ascending vertical or perpendicular strike.

Reciprocal: the lateral hands of opponents facing each other.

Serpentine: spiral, curvative.

Spiral: curve, curvative.

Transversal: the nonlateral hands; right versus right, and left versus left hands of partners facing each other.

Trapezoidal: the method of footwork that results in the shape of a trapezoid.

Triangular: the method of footwork that resembles the shape of a triangle.

Vertex: the top of a triangle whose one side is parallel to the ground.

Vertical: a descending perpendicular strike.

APPENDIX E

Basic Stances and Steps

Advance: a forward position of the right of left foot over the other.

Back Stance: a position where the body weight is more on the hind foot.

Back Step: to step back.

Forward Stance: a position where the body weight is more on the front foot.

Left Oblique: a 45-degree stance with the left foot forward.

Lunge (Attack) Stance: an attack with a forward movement with the weapon hand and the hind foot unmoved but fully extended.

Neutral: a normal, at-ease, nonbelligerent stance.

Oblique Back Stance: a back stance at 45 degrees.

Oblique Back Step: a back step at 45 degrees.

Oblique Forward: a 45-degree forward stance.

Right Oblique: a 45-degree stance with the right foot forward.

Side Step: a step to the left or right side.

Straddle: a position with the feet spread, as when sitting on horseback.

APPENDIX F

Martial Arts Song

Words and music by R.U. Estalilla Jr.

1. Punch and block, or jump and kick—that is what I do;

    As I work out for my gold with the skills I know:

    Strike, fend, or duck and fake, or I'd take you down;

    If you pin me to the ground, man, I'd lose my crown.

REFRAIN:

    Oh, Oh . . . the martial arts . . .

    Yes, we love the fighting arts!

    Here we build up self-esteem, strength, and confidence;

    Here we stand for discipline, friendship, and self-defense;

    We believe . . . in martial arts! Long live . . . the fighting arts!

2. Aikido, Arnis, Judo, Kendo, Karate,

    Wushu, Taichi, Taekwondo, Kungfu, Savate;

    Kickboxing, Combato, Penjak, Jujitsu,

    Kali, Kabaroan, Kenpo, just to name a few

TAMBULI MEDIA

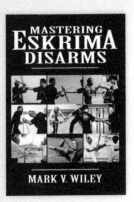

Made in United States
North Haven, CT
20 March 2023

34345277R00098